Living on the Edge
of an Era

Living on the Edge of an Era

RACHEL MORRIS KULP

To order additional copies of this book, contact:
Xlibris Corporation
1-888-795-4274
www.Xlibris.com
Orders@Xlibris.com
36097

Contents

DEDICATION

As I attempted to recover scenes from yesteryear, I came upon this poem written by my mother many years ago. It expresses my motivation coming from the depths of my heart, and my hopes and prayers for everything I write.

THESE WORDS

I pray Thee for heavenly wisdom
That words which I put in rhyme,
May be words that You would have written,
To give help and strength for this time.

May they be words to Thy honor and glory,
To show that I love Thee, my Lord;
That all may see Thee exalted,
As we read and study Thy Word.

So help me to put down the right things
To give out the good, the pure and the strong.
So all may come to trust Jesus,
And forever forsake what is wrong.

By Esther M. Morris

I want my children and grandchildren to visualize and live those times from the past through my stories. This book is dedicated to them and to the memory of my two wonderful parents, Dan and Esther Morris, who guided my life.

INTRODUCTION

Teetering on the brink of yesteryear, we grew up on the edge of an era, an era soon to erupt into expansion in industry, communication and transportation and most importantly—the common access to electricity.

Some called us old-fashioned or backward or uneducated. Certainly not up with the times. But, it was the age we lived in, an age where we saw the future as held by God in His strong, capable hands, and the past as a lesson to be learned.

The challenges, the hopes, the joys were there as we peered through future's window, as we lived on the edge of an era.

DOLL CLOTHES

I was a little girl in the 1940's. We were very poor, and on our farm, we lived in a very small cement block house my father had built. It was so small that the living room, dining room and my bedroom were all in one room. The house was cold, damp and drafty. I slept on the living room sofa along the back wall. The cold metal-framed window above my bed seeped frigid air around my face as I slept. Wild vines outside the window sent scratchy, scary sounds into the night as little rodents scurried up and down among the branches. The one warm spot in the house was the big pot-bellied stove across the room. Sometimes the stove would be so hot that the metal turned fiery red and the big crack in its side opened up so I could see the flames inside.

I used to lie on my cot in our little block house and dream of fancy things like my friends had. Many of them had radios to entertain themselves. Some of my friends had their own bicycles. They had wind-up toys, pretty dolls and new clothes every school year. We did not even have enough money to buy clothes for my dolls.

My dolls all needed new clothes. I even prayed for pretty clothes for my dolls. I asked my Mama for doll clothes, but she said we could not afford them . . . not even fabric to make them. I knew I could make clothes for my dolls if I had the fabric. After all, I was five years old!

One day as I lay on my bed, I saw the answer to my prayers. There on the dining room table was the solution. Such lovely, white fabric was hanging down from the table. It was so rich and silky smooth. How perfect for doll clothes! They would dress my little friends so adorably in frosty white.

One evening while Mama was busy milking the cows, I got out my little scissors. I cut out my doll dresses from that pretty fabric that was just "hanging down." When Mama came in, she cried. Then she spanked me. I didn't understand why she was so angry when I had the prettiest doll dresses anyone could ever want. Later I learned that I had gotten what I prayed for, but I went after the answers the wrong way.

Note: This is a true story that concluded many years later after Mama had passed away. As I was cleaning out drawers in her dining room buffet, I found a stack of very patched, very worn off-white linen tablecloths.

PICKINS

My farmer parents always raised a variety of plants. They had a truck patch with sweet potatoes, squash (yellow and green with white stripes), pumpkins, sweet corn and popcorn. Then was also a garden with wonderful vegetables in it; tomatoes, celery, cabbage, onions, parsley, beans, peppers, salsify and ground cherries. There was not a garden in the area that could compare with the beauty and size of Papa's produce. So, Papa, Mama and we kids hoed and hoed until not a single weed dared raise its head. Mama had her flower gardens. Peonies, Johnny-jump-ups and daffodils bloomed in the spring. She raised Seven-Sister roses that bloomed all summer. She had cosmos that were "volunteers," hollyhocks and Snow-on-the Mountain. Sometimes I carried cuddly-soft pussy willow kitkins from the tree by the chicken house in my little apron pocket.

When I was three and a half, the round, bursting buds on the peonies attracted my attention. There was something mysterious about their closed round firmness that I couldn't resist. I found a zinc jar lid, the kind Mama used for canning. It was just the right size for my hand.

There was a peony bush behind my bedroom window . . . with those bursting buds waving at me. They were just the right height for me to touch with my nose. Ah, they smelled good! I wanted to keep them, always and always. So, I picked one and put it in my little lid. Then I picked another. I picked until I filled that little jar lid, and there were no more buds. They packed in so nicely. I proudly carried it to my Mama.

I just couldn't understand why she wasn't happy, and why she took my peony buds away.

"Why, Mama?" My tears made rivulets down my cheeks.

The bush came back the next year with many more beautiful blooms. And I have wonderful fragrant memories that have bloomed in my heart down through the years.

THE ALADDIN LAMP

With great regret and tender memories, I placed the old Aladdin lamp in the trash box. I could no longer get parts for it. The metal chrome was peeling and rusted. The frosted glass shade had been stained in the walnut-logged water of Papa's basement. A large chunk had broken out of the glass shade.

My Mama's hands had touched that lamp, had lit that lamp each night. I miss her and I remember . . .

I was four years old. Every night Mama would go out to feed, water and milk the cows. She had to shovel out the manure, such back-breaking work. Papa was out on the tractor, farming. Mama would smell of the barn, the odor of manure mixed with warm milk and fresh hay until she took off her milking clothes. To me, Mama smelled just wonderful because she was my Mama.

We had no electricity. I used to sit on my little chair (a potty chair with the lid on) and wait for Mama to come in and light that Aladdin lamp. It grew dark as evening fell. I heard scary, scratchy noises in the vines that entwined our three-room cement-block house. Unknown animals scrambled up and down against the metal window frame. Sometimes I would hear winds from a storm. On my little chair, I would scoot back all the way under the hot water reservoir of the kitchen wood cook stove where I thought I would be safe. No one could see me, and the noises in the dark couldn't find me there.

Mama would come soon. I knew she would. But it was so scary, all alone in the dark. Then, when Mama did come in from the barn and lit that old Aladdin lamp, everything was all right.

MUD PIES

When I was a little girl, I delighted in making mud pies and presenting them to my mother. She graciously accepted them and always asked how I made them. I told her they were made with a secret ingredient, which I told no one. Now, long after Mama passed on, I am revealing my secret.

The first step was to find a pile of used, gray, zinc jar lids. They were just the right size for a one-serving pie. I would carry them to the barn and wipe them out with a fistful of fresh straw.

In the front corner of our red barn, near the heavy sliding barn door, sat what my Papa proudly called "The Hammermill." I don't know if that was its brand name or a description of what it did. It was a large red contraption about five feet long with a wide spout at the top in which grain was roughly hammered into meal to feed our herd of cattle. One day as I examined "Mr. Hammer," I found a little handle at the bottom. It opened a small round door that I had never noticed before. Inside that little door was a mound of ground grain. What a treasure I had found! I don't think Papa ever knew I had found it.

To make my pies, I filled my little pie pans with ground meal and added soupy mud juice from the nearest mud hole, just enough to make a cream cheese consistency. I usually strained out the bugs and debris from the mud unless I decided I wanted an extra crunchy texture. The final step was a garnish of wild carrot flower top or a sprig of clover leaves with a white blossom on top. The pies were then placed on a board and carried to a sunny spot to bake.

When the each center was set, I would offer a pie to my dog, Trixie. If she liked my pies, she would lick the edges clean. After her approval, I offered the prettiest of the pies to my mother. If Mama "Ah'd" and "Oh'd" over my pies, I knew I had done a good job. Perhaps I would decide to open my own bakery some day and share my goodies with the world.

THE BLOOMERS

I did not like my first grade teacher. She took away my red pencil that I was using to color my nails. I wanted them to be pretty like those of my classmates who wore bright red nail polish. When my pencil was returned, someone else had chewed on it and made it three inches shorter. That was during my first week of school.

For the whole year, I remember going to school wearing hand-me-downs. That would not have been a problem if they had not been handed down from four older cousins first. One thing that was not handed down was the stockings—ugly, ribbed brown ones. All of the other girls had pretty, white, long stockings. Everyone knew we were poor because the brown ones were the cheapest. I had to sit in the center of the front row for our school picture in my ugly, brown, long stockings, surrounded by all the other girls in their new white stockings.

Mama economized the best she could. She made my underwear. Granted, other people were not supposed to know what your underwear looked like, but the other girls knew. Sometimes, for fun, they would pull up my skirt and . . .

"Look, Sissy has bloomers! Come and see!"

"Ha, ha," The girls doubled over with laughter.

My Mama made them out of flour sacks, plain off-white muslin ones with lumps in the fabric. She thought Red Rose made the best flour so Red Rose sacks were the most plentiful. My bloomers were long, to be modest, reaching down to my knees. There was elastic at the knees and elastic at the waist. I was so embarrassed to wear those ugly bloomers. I wanted to be dressed in store-bought underwear like the other girls.

One wintry day was the only day I was ever thankful that Mama made me wear snow pants. As I stepped off the school bus, the elastic around my waist broke. I tried to hurry in my fallen state, but with the underwear around my ankles, I could barely waddle up the long driveway to our house. The other students on the bus did not realize what had happened inside my snow pants, but whatever it was surely looked funny on the outside.

I fell into Mama's waiting arms, consumed by sobs. Finally, I was calm enough to tell her what had happened. After that, the ugly bloomers were recycled. I don't remember ever having to wear them again.

MAMA'S MEDICINE CABINET

When I got sick, Mama or her maiden aunties always had a remedy. Sometimes the remedy was worse than the sickness. Her concoctions always prompted me to get well quickly.

The first and worst remedy I remember was the onion poultice. If I had a chest cold, Mama would put me to bed early. Then she would fry a batch of onions in lard until they were soft and greasy. She would place the smelly mess on my chest as I lay on my back. Then she would fasten a small sheet or towel all around me and secure it with safety pins. She would tell me good night and leave to let the poultice do its job. It actually seemed to help except that, when I turned on my side to sleep in the middle of the night, the onions would slide off to my side. I would, for sure, be better the next morning and be sent to school. Since we only had a bath on Saturday nights, all my school mates knew what remedy Mama had tried.

As we became more modern, Mama smeared Vicks Vaporub all over my chest and throat and covered it with a pinned-on towel. Before I went to bed, she made a tent of newspapers over a bowl. The bowel contained a glob of Vicks. I put my head under the tent and breathed as Mama poured boiling water from the teakettle into the bowl. It did clear my stuffy nose.

When Papa had a stuffy nose, he would pour some pink powder called Vince into the palm of his hand and sniff it into his nose. He claimed it was the best stuff. He declared black Carbonic Salve was the cure-all for splinters and skin infections.

Mama had a cure for about everything in her medicine cabinet. She made juniper berry tea for female problems and sent me to bed. She prescribed Lydia Pinkhams for female problems and Carters Little Liver Pills for constipation. She would administer a big tablespoon of caster oil to me if she suspected I was getting sick from anything. I got well fast. She would slather a blob of butter over a burn. Of course later we learned that was the worst thing to do, but she did what her aunties had done before her. Sometimes she would smear mustard over the burn first to "take the fire out." Papa said a tablespoon of blackstrap molasses would cure anything. It depended upon which parent got to me first to cure me.

When we had an earache, Mama would heat sweet oil and pour it into our ear. We had to lie on the other side while the oil trickled into our ear, then turn and drain it out. When we had a cold, Mama would fill a hot water bottle and apply it to our chest while we were in bed. Or, she might make us sit on a chair with our feet in a pan full of hot Epsom Salts water.

In cold weather, she would wrap up a brick or flat iron that had heated on the stove in newspaper and put it down by our feet. She claimed that if our feet were warm, we were warm.

THE "O's" IN MY MILK

Mama usually cooked breakfast for Papa and me. Once in a while Papa would make it. We always had cooked cereal—oatmeal, cream of wheat, malt-o-meal or cornmeal mush. With hot cereal, we were served pancakes, toast, bacon and often scrambled eggs and Ovaltine to drink. We used our own whole milk, fresh from the cow. Papa liked to add an extra half-cup of rich cream to his cereal on top of the milk. He'd wink and call it his "candy." (Years later, after Papa sold his cows, he would eat his cereal with powdered skim milk and a double serving of canned evaporated milk on top. I'm glad I didn't have to do that!)

One morning when I was about seven, Mama told me she and Papa had agreed to let me spend the night at my Aunt Stella's house. Aunt Stella and Uncle Harmon lived almost a mile down the road. My cousin, who was seven years older, let me stay with her in her pretty room.

My aunt's house was so different than our little three-room cement block house. It had two stories, and its clean white paint made it seem so huge. When I stepped inside the kitchen, there was no barnyard odor from milking clothes hung beside the door. Her house smelled of fresh lilacs. Long, lacy curtains hung crisply at the windows. Aunt Stella's handmade doilies adorned backs and arms of chairs and under every plant. Everything was neatly in its place, unlike our house. There was no clutter anywhere.

I had never slept in such a wonderful bed—crisp, white sheets, big, fluffy pillows with embroidered lacy covers. After the bright morning sun smiled through our bedroom window, we went downstairs for breakfast.

We all bowed our heads and held hands as Uncle Harmon said the blessing.

"Rachel," he asked, "would you like to try some Cheerios?"

I had never tasted cold cereal before. Uncle poured a bowl of Cheerios. Then he poured milk out of a box and added sugar. I wondered if it was okay to eat milk that came from a box. Where was the cow? I really enjoyed this different kind of breakfast, right down to the last "O" in the milk as I finished my second bowl.

WOOD BEES

I liked to watch my Papa working with wood. He had set up a couple of sawhorses in the front yard and was planing boards for a project. His hands skillfully moved the plane up and down the log, making long, sweet-smelling curls of wood strips. At six years of age, those curls fascinated me. I used to string them together and dance in a circle as they trailed behind me.

Then, I had a great idea. I took several of the longest curls and fastened them under the band of my straw hat. Now, instead of having reddish brown hair, I was a curly blonde. I ran through the yard, my new blonde curls bobbing in the sunlight. They made me feel special.

Suddenly, I heard a buzzing. A big bumble bee had smelled the wood strips. A second bee joined him, and a third, a fourth and more. B-z-z-z, b-z-z-z. Terrified, I ran across the yard. They followed those bouncing curls. And, they were angry!

"Help, help!" I screamed, running, and crying all at the same time.

Mama, who was working in the garden, heard my wails. Immediately she saw the problem. "Take off your hat!" she commanded.

I threw my beautiful hat to the ground and ran sobbing into her comforting arms. Somehow, I never felt like playing with wood curls again.

FROM 1943 ON . . .

I was very young when World War II changed our lives. I really didn't understand the looks of horror on adult faces after the bombing of Pearl Harbor. I did sense an urgency and restlessness. Although we worked on our farm as usual, there were a multitude of changes.

Many women answered the appeal of "Rosie the Riveter" or the pointed finger of "Uncle Sam Wants You," and rushed to work in the factories turning out wartime goods. They wore pants, rolled up their sleeves, and tackled jobs formerly held by men. My Mama had plenty to do helping Papa on the farm. In her faded work apron and cotton dresses, she worked as hard as any factory lady. Besides, gasoline was rationed which would have made travel to town to work every day very difficult.

Many items of daily use were in short supply. The OPA (Office of Price Administration) began cycling common items to the military. I noticed Mama wearing "holey" hose when we went to church. Nylon stockings were only available to military women. Mama felt it was proper to wear stockings, holes or not.

People applied for ration tokens and ration booklets to help them purchase items in short supply like sugar, butter, coffee and gasoline. I remember Mama scolding me when I found the little red ration tokens in the bottom of her purse and started playing with them. I certainly didn't understand why she was angry—something about only having enough tokens for ten pounds of sugar in peach-canning season.

Instead of butter, we used oleo (like margarine) which we prepared every two weeks. Mama would purchase a bag of white "grease" and the packet of reddish-colored seasoning which came with it. We mixed them together to make a more palatable yellow-colored spread.

Mama would go to her piano and hammer out songs like, "On the Road to Mandalay (where the flying fishes play)," "When It's Springtime in the Rockies (I'll be coming back to you)" and "Just Like the Sunrise" to cheer herself when everything looked so gloomy.

It was a time of national pride but also of social and racial unrest. There was discrimination against the blacks and against Japanese citizens who were sent to relocation camps. Race riots erupted in many cities. During this time, organizations like the Congress of Racial Equality and the National Association for the Advancement of Colored People were born. Papa would read about these things in The Defiance Crescent News. He was especially upset at the Italians. I would hear him mumbling about Mussolini although I didn't have the faintest idea who Mussolini was. He blamed them for many of the problems. I certainly didn't understand about those things and didn't care. We, in our little farming community, were quite isolated from the terrors of war. I do remember listening to our static-filled radio as President Roosevelt give his fireside chats. His Four Freedoms for America sounded so eloquent and hope filled.

Eventually the Axis nations surrendered to the Allies and the war was over. Our neighbor soldier boys came home. Finally, our nation could get back to our normal daily living.

THE OTHER GRANDMOTHER

My first memories of Grandmother Morris, my Papa's mother, were when I was about six years old. Grandfather had died shortly before I was born. They lived in Putnam County, near North Creek, Ohio.

My first impressions of her house made me frightened. We had come to the old homestead for a family dinner. The house seemed dark and foreboding to my little eyes. I clung to Mama's hand when we entered. The front steps led directly into the dining room where a large table was set for twelve. To the left and a part of the room was the kitchen. Grandmother would cook over a very large, very black cookstove. There were benches lining the walls and a work table in the center of the kitchen. A stack of feed sack towels was neatly folded on an open shelf beside the cast-iron skillets and aluminum cooking pots. Because the family belonged to the Brethren in Christ Church, there were no frills in her kitchen or on her person.

To the right was Grandmother's bedroom. I remember her lying on her lumpy bed when she was "sick-a-bed." The room was very plain: a bed, a chair, a washbasin and pitcher on a wash stand. Everything was gray or dingy white, even the curtains. The straw mattress, the striped pillow ticking, everything smelled of sickness.

Since Grandmother was old and sickly, it was my Mama's job to take turns with the other family members caring for her, even though it was Papa's side of the family. Mama was supposed to go once a month to help, but when others couldn't do their part, she ended up helping every other week. When Grandmother was bedfast, Mama would have to turn her and treat her bedsores. There were no antibiotics. Mama did the best she could. Mama would cook the evening meal, then wash and change the bedding in that dingy, smelly room. I busied myself with the cats at the back door or looked for books to read.

One afternoon when Grandmother was feeling better and walking about, Mama was in her bedroom changing the bedding, emptying the bedpan and shaking the rugs. Mama had just made a nice supper of roast beef, mashed potatoes and gravy with string beans. I was looking forward to the meal. My mouth had watered when she cooked it.

Somehow, when Mama's back was turned, Grandmother got past her and went into the kitchen. Now Grandmother's mind was not what it used to be so she decided it was time to make supper. I'll never forget her standing at the stove in her long gray dress with white apron, her thin gray hair pulled back in a tight bun. She was a tall, thin woman who was never a warm, cuddly, friendly grandmother. She was stern and austere. I was afraid of her and had to be prodded to speak to her.

I remember her standing there "making supper." First, she added the gravy to the mashed potatoes. Then she chopped the roast beef and the string beans and added them to the potatoes. Then she stirred. How she stirred! She was still stirring when Mama finished the bedroom and found her. Mama was angry! Our supper that night was a treat only for those of the family who had false teeth.

GRANDPA'S CLOCK

Sometimes Papa, Mama and I would pile into the car along with Mama's basket of freshly baked pies. We were going to my Papa's old home place. Grandpa M had died, but Papa's sisters and their families would gather once a year to have a family dinner with Grandma M.

The family table seated at least twenty. I remember chipped brown stoneware plates and silver-plated, well-worn forks and spoons. The cut glass goblets would have been pretty, but years of washing in black sulfur water made them look grimy. Papa's sisters were very good cooks, and soon we were totally stuffed. I helped Mama clear the table, but was shooed from the kitchen when it got too crowded.

There was no one my age to play with as I was the youngest cousin. Some of the men would retire to the study and sit in the huge leather chairs. I would choose the overstuffed horsehair sofa because I could slide around on it. I had to watch out for the worn spots where the broken leather would scratch my legs.

All of a sudden the mantel clock on top of the bookshelf would chime. "Bong . . . bong . . . bong." Reverberating against the ceiling, the noise was deafening. I rushed, terrified, from the room and into Mama's arms. Later, I would come back to my seat when the clock had finished. It looked so enormous sitting up there on the shelf.

There was an oak roll-top desk in that room. Rumor was that the desk had a hidden compartment. Perhaps there was an envelope of money or jewels hidden there. No one had been able to find it.

Years later, after Grandpa M died, I found the old desk stored on the top floor of Papa's open corn crib, exposed to wind and weather. I persuaded Papa to give it to me for Christmas one year. We took the desk apart. The hidden compartment really was there. It had no money in it, only receipted bills.

As for the clock, it disappeared for many years. One day I found it in Mama's wash room in her very wet basement. It was warped and falling apart. Mama gave it to me for my birthday. We cleaned, glued and polished that clock until it looked like new. It proudly sits on my shelf where it doesn't look nearly as big as it did then.

PICTURE DAY

The second grade was my most awful year of school. My teacher was Mrs. Gossler. I never liked her, but I did try hard to please her. She frowned at most of us girls at least once a day. She used to flick our hands with her pencil if we weren't writing. I think she either started each day with a bad breakfast or else she was just too old to enjoy us kids. One day Mrs. Gossler announced that the day after next would be picture day.

My aunt was a hair dresser. She said I should have curly hair for my picture just like the other girls. On the night before picture day, she decided to give me a permanent wave. Hair perms were not well tested at that time. There were hot waves and cold waves. She selected a cold wave because she thought it would last longer. My aunt then rolled my hair onto tiny metal rollers about one quarter inch thick with rows of little holes on them. The perm lotion smelled terrible. My hair was so hot it sizzled! Why, oh why it was called a cold wave?

Finally, the rollers came out. I had curls, but I was so disappointed. Instead of the shiny, bouncy curls my friends had, my hair was hanging in pencil-tight, dried, crimped ringlets. They didn't bounce. They just hung like stiff, tiny bottle scrubbers.

The next morning I wanted to wear my favorite dress. It was bright red with little white flowers dancing across the front. After Mama ran it through her wringer washer, it came out looking like a faded rag. My second grade picture shows a scared little rabbit with big buck teeth, stringy hair, faded dress and long brown stockings in the center front row.

WATCHING STARS

On a bright, star-lit October evening, around 8:00 or 9:00 o'clock after all the chores were done, Mama would say to me, "Put on your coat. Let's take a walk."

Gladly, I'd slip my little hand inside her warm, work-worn one, and we'd head out the back door. We would pass the chicken house, the pig pen and Papa's peach trees to our spot where the stars shone brightest. The night would be spangled with the light of a billion stars. There wasn't any smog then because there wasn't any General Motors or other big factory nearby.

We would start with Polaris, the North Star, to get our bearings and wander around the sky; the twins, Castor and Pollock, Andromeda reclining in her chair, the Big and Little Dippers. Mama had her favorite constellations which she would point out to me. My favorite was Orion and then Taurus with the cluster of Pleiades nearby. I thought Orion was so brave, keeping watch every night over the sky. Mama's favorite star was Sirius, the brightest star that was sometimes called the Dog Star, and after that, red Betelgeuse and Arcturus and Vega. She would name others, and I would try to find them before she did, stars like: Capella, Aldebaran, Rigel and Procyon. Those stars were easy to spot with the naked eye, and we didn't have a telescope. I just looked for the constellation they were in. After we looked at the stars and constellations, we would count the planets to make sure they were still there where God had hung them. Long ago Mama had taught me that stars twinkle and planets just shine.

Some evenings Mama and I would head out the front door and look north. The aurora borealis would drop down like a shimmering curtain. Luminous colors like silvers, turquoise and rose shifted to reds, greens and blues as the curtains moved up and down and side to side like giant ribbons in the wind. We would "ah" and "oh" at the sight. It was better than fireworks.

Then Mama would say, "It's getting cold out here. Let's go in." The show was over for the night.

CHASING BLACKIE

I used to think of cows as my friends when I was growing up. They seemed to be such large creatures to a little girl. They were pretty with their gentle brown eyes and their soft, hairy coats. Their tongues, when they licked my hand, had lots of little prickles that tickled me and made me giggle. Most of our cows had curved horns that they knew how to use when anyone got in their way.

One of the prettiest and also the smallest of the cows was the Jersey, Blackie. She was as black as her name implied, inside and out. She was very smart and stubborn and would lie down in her stantion when Papa tried to milk her. She just did not like to be milked. Then she would flick him in the eyes with her tail. That would make Papa angry, so he would fasten her tail under his knee. She would pull back against the restraints and roll her eyes at him. She would have hung herself rather than submit to a human.

Good examples of Jersey devising were their Sunday morning performances. Blackie was the ringleader. She and her buddies knew exactly when we were dressed in our Sunday clothes and ready to leave for church. It usually happened when we were running late and scrambling to get into the car. Someone would notice, "Oh, no! The cows are out!" Or, one of our kind neighbors would phone us that our cows were "trampling her garden, and would we get them out right now!"

We would have to stop what we were doing and chase those stupid (or not-so-stupid) cows. I believe they had a bovine sense of humor. We would either be late for church from having to change clothes again or arrive late and very, very dirty.

We raised mostly registered Jersey cows, that is, with a couple of brown Gurnseys thrown in. Papa often said that Jerseys were the smartest breed of cows. They outsmarted us many times, but their milk was the richest and best which made it worth the effort of chasing them.

MAMA'S POEMS

From the long line of artistic people in the Myers family line, my great Aunt Edna was the artist, and my Mama was a poet and story teller. She wrote over one hundred and ten poems, some of them were finished after she was old and in the nursing home. Their dates ranged from the forties through the mid-nineties when she died. The sad thing was that Mama didn't have the money needed to publish her works. She sat in her overstuffed chair in the evenings when the work was done, writing. She wrote about her cats, her children, her family and about how much she loved her Lord. The church secretary printed many of them, and they appeared weekly in the church bulletin. I have chosen to reprint a few of her poems. It is the only way Mama will be "published."

OCTOBER

Over the hills and the valleys,
October's blue haze lies.
The goldenrod so yellow,
With flaming maple vies.

The trees in apple orchards
With fruit are hanging low,
They promise pies for winter,
And a snack when cold winds blow.

We gather from the garden
A store of goodly things,
The squash, the corn, the onions,
A feast from harvest brings.

Our feet go through the brown leaves,
A lovely rustling sound,
We scatter them about us,
To find nuts upon the ground.

The nights are coming chilly,
Though days are warm and bright,
A golden moon above us
Sets all the land alight.

Oh, golden days of autumn,
Could you forever stay!
You are best of all the seasons,
October's bright blue day!

By Esther M. Morris
Used by permission of Susan Newton.

Mama's birthday was in October. Two of her granddaughters were also born in October. She wrote this poem in their honor to "Us October Girls:"

*　　*　　*

THE SAILOR BROTHER

Oh, Sailor Brother, where are you tonight?
Under a dark, murky sky,
    Riding the white waves high,
    Surging, rising, sullen and slow;
As your prow rears high, then plunges low,
Are you there in the misty night?.

Sailor Brother, did you pass
Cities and ports on a distant shore?
    Did your ship sail into a foreign clime,
    Or battle the high waves more and more?
Sailor Brother, where are you tonight,
Standing the watch in the dismal night?

May heaven guide your bark tonight,
As winds and storms your deck assail.
    May the good God guard and protect your ship
    As it weathers the sleet, the hail and the gale!
I'd follow its wake, were your ship in sight,
Oh, Sailor Brother, where are you tonight?

By Esther M. Morris
From "My Own Poems" collection

Mama's brother, my Uncle Paul, was a ship captain on the Great Lakes. This was written for him.

*   *   *

SEPARATION

I do not wish to hold you
It is time that you must go.
Life lays its goals before you,
That your rightful place may know.

I would not keep you near me,
Lest it mar the Father's will.
His hand will guide you safely,
As you His work fulfill.

As you trust Him for His leading,
As He opens up your way,
We'll be happy that no hindrance
Held you from His will this day.

To tell you "Go" is not easy,
Heartstrings draw and mem'ries bind,
But I would not choose your future,
For 'tis yours His will to find.

Long ago we gave you to Him
And we'd never think to dare
Ever to rescind our promise
Or to doubt God's loving care.

So tho' we'll not be close together,
There is love, and its strong cord,
And our mutual faith in Jesus,
Unites us through His living Word.

We commend you to His keeping,
May we all e'er faithful be,
Till there breaks the Light of Heaven,
Through the glad eternity.

Esther M. Myers Morris
From "My Own Poems" collection

My Mother wrote this poem as I left home to be married and start a new life far away. I am sure this is the heart cry of every mother as her children leave home.

*　　*　　*

MY LORD SPEAKS

The way seems rough—"I know, my child,
It is painful, weary and slow.
Yet for your sake and to My glory
This is the way I'd have you to go.

You know I promise to give you strength,
I'll always be by your side.
Stay close by Me, I'm always there,
In my love You may surely abide.

Just let your faith go soaring high
For it will bring you through;
Your faith, My promises and My love
In abundance I have for you.

The dark, discouraging days will pass.
The clouds will break, My light will shine.
For when all the troubles and trials are gone,
You'll be in heaven, forever Mine."

By Esther M. Morris
From "My Own Poems" collection

This poem shows a premonition of what problems Mother would have in the future as her health deteriorated. This is probably one of the last poems she was able to write in longhand.

RATS AND FEATHERS

Carefully little Rachel scooped the dirt from the side of the ditch to form a little hole. Then she planted her "plant," mounding the sandy topsoil around it and patting it down with chubby little hands. That night as Mama listened to her prayers, she heard,

"And Jesus, please make that feather grow that I planted."

*   *   *

Things were tough for farmers in northwestern Ohio. It was in the mid-forties and coccidiosis as well as other diseases swept through the chicken houses. Laying hens fell dead by the dozens. We tried to get medicine into the chickens either by food or by water.

My Mama and I struggled with big three-gallon jugs of Blue Vitrol that Mama expertly flipped into the watering trays. I tried to flip one like Mama did, but my seven-year-old arms couldn't control the heavy bottle. Just before it crashed to the floor, Mama caught the floundering jug and plopped it into position.

In the spring we would get several large, flat boxes with punched-out holes in the mail. The postman would call ahead to be sure we were home to receive them. Soft peeping sounds came through the holes. If we shook the boxes, the sounds became a clamor. Inside were the soft, yellow bodies of white leghorn chicks. I loved to hold the peeps next to my cheek, their downy fuzz tickling my nose. Each one felt like a living drop of sunshine.

We had built special incubator brooder houses for the babies, complete with heaters and lights. Special care was taken to make the floors solid to keep out predators. My job was to check on the babies before going to bed. I made sure they had mash and water, the right temperature, and that the door was closely sealed.

When the babies grew into layers, we moved them into the big chicken house. There were roosts for the chickens at night and lots of straw underneath where they could hide their eggs. I helped Mama gather eggs. I thought it was fun to find the little white treasures in the straw, being careful not to step on any of them. Once in a while, a mother hen would scold me and flap her wings at me or peck me when I reached under her. I don't blame her. I was invading her privacy.

When I was about ten, I was big enough to help Mama clean the chicken house. She and I wore red kerchiefs tied across our noses whenever we entered the chicken house to change the bedding. At times we had to scrape the roosts with flat paddles. If rats got into the hen house, the droppings could cause disease, so we had to clean very thoroughly. How I hated the smell and grit of chicken dust in the air: the feathers, the straw, the dander and droppings. We also had to clean thoroughly or the chickens would get larnygostasis, a coughing disease caused from uncleanness. We had to spray with a mixture containing Rotenone to prevent lice and mites. Chickens would pick each others' lice and became cannibals once they drew blood. I remember dabbing the poor injured chickens' behinds with tar to prevent others from pecking them. Many times they did not survive. Often when we swept the roosts and floor, the dust was too thick for us to see each other. Our hair, eyelashes and kerchiefs would be almost white with dust and dander. Mama and I would cough and sneeze. Sometimes I thought she would never stop sneezing. Then, for weeks, she would cough deep, hacking coughs. I didn't know she had chronic bronchitis. All I knew was that we must tend those chickens.

We began to notice less and less eggs being harvested. We wondered why. Where were they going? Mother hens didn't usually eat their eggs. But more and more eggs were missing.

One day while I was in the storage area in the lower level, I heard strange, squealing sounds. What was going on? The sounds came from a large wooden vinegar barrel where Mama had stored some quilts and old winter clothing. Carefully, I peered in—I saw movement and heard more squeals. Rats! That's what were in that barrel. But now what were we going to do about the problem? Papa was away, working in the fields. Mama was deathly afraid of rats. I decided to be brave.

Now, how could I do this? I didn't want to watch them die. I didn't want the rats to jump up out of the barrel in my face. I had a plan. I selected several heavy, wide boards and covered the top of the barrel with them. Then I found a broom handle with the broom part broken off. I stuck the handle into the barrel between the boards and started pounding. I stomped and pounded for all I was worth. The rats squealed—a horrible high-pitched, shrieking sound. I couldn't imagine a barrel of rats could be so loud. As I pounded, once in a while I would hear one jump and hit the top of the barrel. That would make me jump, but I kept on pounding and pounding. Finally, all of the squealing stopped. The barrel stopped wiggling inside. I didn't have the courage to look at their dead, battered bodies.

I think Papa probably emptied that barrel. At least the next day it was empty. We had a great "crop" of eggs after that. And, God did bless the feather that I planted!

OUR CHRISTMAS BOX

Christmas was coming and all of Defiance County was dressing itself in gaudy late 40's trimmings. The war was over, and the nation felt like celebrating. Yet at our house, there would be few gifts and not much celebration. Decorations would be the same ragged ornaments worn out from many years of use.

"Teenteen (Mama's nickname for me), run up to the attic and fetch the box," Mama's voice echoed into my upstairs room.

"What box, Mama?" I asked.

I rushed down the stairs. Mama was stirring a corn pudding for Christmas. Corn was about all we had to eat.

"You know what box." Mama frowned. "The Christmas box."

"Oh, Mama!"

Horrible thoughts raced through my brain. That dirty, dingy, musty, old attic! I would have to crawl between boxes, under the beams, with cobwebs tangling my hair and dangling in my eyes. And, it was so dark up there. Like all ten-year old girls, I detested dirt, bugs, and screechy, scratchy noises on attic windows.

I did know what box Mama meant. It was a large, round cheese box, packed with crumpled Christmas wrapping paper Mama had saved from years of Christmases past. She would carefully unwrap her gifts, and we unwrapped ours, being careful not to rip the stickers, carefully smoothing out the paper to be stored for the next year or years to come. Sometimes when we dug through the box, we'd see tags from Christmas gifts years ago. Why couldn't we buy new wrapping paper like all of my friends' families did! I knew very well why. Our crops had failed for the last several years. Our savings were gone. We were dirt poor.

I needed a gift for my friend Aileen for our class party. She liked nice things and I wanted a Christmas gift that would please her. What could I give her when I didn't even have an allowance?

"Now, where is that box?"

I found the box. A thick layer of dust crusted the top.

"Ugh, it's heavy," I muttered.

What is this bag crushed underneath it? Yes, I remember. My Aunt Catharine gave me this shawl. Long fringes edged the soft green wool. I never wore it. I had no clothes that would go with a shawl. I brought the bag down with the box.

"Look, Mama, I found Aunt Catharine's shawl." I pulled the bag open.

It was the week of Christmas and the class party. Mama dug through the Christmas box and wrapped gifts for our family. I still had no gift for Aileen.

"Why don't you give your friend the shawl from Aunt Catharine? She wouldn't mind." Mama suggested.

"But Mama, how shall I wrap it? I want it to be pretty."

"Well, we have plenty of wrapping paper in this box," Mama said firmly.

I found the best-looking piece of wrapping paper and smoothed out the wrinkles the best I could. It was covered with Santas and pink reindeer.

At the party the gifts were handed out. I dreaded seeing Aileen's face when she saw the shabbily wrapped gift. Immediately Aileen ripped off the paper.

"Oh, Christine, this is the best present I ever received."

"Why . . . how . . ." I stammered.

"Don't you remember", Aileen squealed. "My last name is Schall. You gave me a gift just like my name. Oh, how I love you!" Squeezing me with her biggest hug, Aileen exclaimed, "You are my very best friend."

The next day, I carried the Christmas box back to the attic for another Christmas.

(Names have been changed and events modified.)

ABOUT MY NEIGHBOR

Halloween was a scary time. At least my friend Aileen and I tried to be scary. We dressed up in costumes and walked to the various neighbors, expecting a treat.

"Trick or treat," we'd shout as we banged on their doors.

My neighbor, Mr. Brakebill, didn't answer the door. We pounded on the door again, louder this time. Finally, in exasperation, we agreed. He didn't want to give us a treat. He deserves a terrible trick. I found an ear of field corn in my coat pocket, left over from feeding our pig. I shelled off the kernels and sprinkled them all over his porch, particularly in front of the door.

That night as I lay on my bed, the guilt feelings hit. Mr. Brakebill was an old man. What if he fell on the corn and hurt himself. Then the trick would all be on me. It was many weeks before I had the nerve to speak to my neighbor, and I never told him what I did.

* * *

Northwestern Ohio is very flat. The closest thing to a hill near our property was the little six foot rise in the wheat field down the road. We used to try to sled down that slope. At the end of our road, where it intersected with Route 15, was a deep drainage ditch. At the corner of the intersection, the ditch was L-shaped and about eight feet deep.

When there was an accident in our community, everyone turned out to look at the scene. We heard there was an awful accident at the Route 15 intersection. We had just had an ice storm so we figured someone missed the stop sign. When we arrived at the scene, there was Mr. Brakebill's battered 1932 Model A Ford sitting head first in that drainage ditch. It was almost vertical. Fortunately, he wasn't hurt badly. It did give the community something to talk about for a long time.

OLD TOM

Sixth graders aren't afraid of much of anything. I was in the sixth grade, and we were on a band trip—all dressed up in our blue and gold uniforms with gold braid on the shoulders, complete with white shirts and black ties. Our band was performing in the annual fall area music competition. Three hours before the next performance, five of us decided to explore downtown Napoleon, Ohio.

"Come over here!" The friendly funeral director motioned us inside his door. Bravely we went. I couldn't remember ever being in a funeral home before.

"I want to show you something," he motioned. "Follow me."

With great hesitation, we followed him through room after room of caskets and vaults. Spooky, very spooky! I thought.

"Follow me up the ladder."

I wondered if we were being kidnapped and held for ransom or just going to mysteriously disappear. Dumbly we clambered up an old, rickety ladder into the attic. Light streaked through cracks in the walls, igniting dust motes floating in the air. Overhead a lone light bulb lit the room.

"Over here." He beckoned.

To our right was a simple, long wooden box. And, there he lay, dressed in baggy brown pants, his dirty, torn white shirt open down the front with a rope for a belt around his waist. The undertaker told us his name was Old Tom. Tom was a vagrant, found along the railroad tracks. He literally drank himself to death and preserved his own body with alcohol.

"It's all right to touch him. Go ahead," we were assured.

He was hard as a rock. His teeth shone permanently fixed in a silly grin. His skin was brown, taut over a bony skeleton. He had hair on his chin and chest. I touched his chest hair carefully. It felt like fine steel wire. He lay there, unseeing, in his box—forever petrified.

We climbed down the ladder and soberly left the mortuary, vowing never, never, never to touch a drink of alcohol.

UNCLE CAPTAIN

"**I** was a sailor-man once," proclaimed my little cousin who was three years younger than I. We were both looking at my Uncle Paul's picture on the wall, nestled in its wide gilded white frame. A cheerful, dignified face with sparkling eyes and soft white beard looked down at us. His navy uniform glittered with gold braid, set off by his white captain's hat. I laughed because my cousin was a "land-lubber." Uncle Paul was the sailor-man. He was a ship captain on the Great Lakes.

Uncle Paul wore many hats. He loved to work on his farm, plowing, seeding, harvesting. He liked to boat or fish in his lake at the end of the day. My Mama and Papa and I always thought he was rich to have a lake and a boat.

He raised at least one thousand geese on his farm. I remember trying to walk through the sea of geese to the lake. Once they decided to block the pathway, no one could go through. They hissed, and they spat. They tried to beat us with their strong wings. Uncle Paul said if they grabbed you with their beaks, they would never let go. All of those heads and long necks swayed and turned like a field of tall white grass. And the squawking . . . it was deafening! It was quite an adventure to retrieve eggs from a protective mother goose. Uncle was proud of his long-necked watchdogs. He and my aunt spent long night hours cleaning and separating the eggs for market.

Uncle Paul had no daughter so I was "his girl." He allowed me to help with his farm chores. It was so much fun to learn something new from him. He taught me Indian lore. I was intrigued by his huge collection of arrowheads, war axes and hammers. It was rumored that we had an Indian ancestor. When I asked Uncle about it, he would just smile and wink. It was a taboo subject.

Uncle Paul raised sugar beets. He built a little village of temporary frame houses to house the migrant workers who tilled and harvested the beets. Many of them spoke no English. Uncle helped me learn Spanish so I could converse with them. We ate lots and lots of sugar beets in those days, so many that I still turn up my nose at them. My "Tio Pablo" kept giving my parents more and more beets plus rutabagas and turnips.

One day he called me down to his basement.

"Come over here," he said. I went over to see what appeared to be miniature corn kernels enclosed in individual husks about one-half inch long clustered on tiny corn cobs.

"This is Indian corn, prehistoric Indian corn. This is a sample developed from ancient seeds."

"Wow!" I thought. "Something that old!"

"I'm going to give these seeds to you," he stated. "I won't be able to do any more with them. Take care of them."

Sadly, I didn't take care of the seeds. I regret not protecting them from the mice that reduced them to miniature corn cobs. A little bit of Uncle Paul was lost.

Uncle Paul was an eighth grade teacher. He was always curious about life. As a child, he got his head stuck in the butter churn, trying to see how it worked.

He was my surrogate papa, ready and willing to give me away at my wedding. His home was my home. No one could ever replace the spot he holds in my heart. My wonderful, sometimes wacky, lovable Uncle Paul.

GRANDPA'S HAIR TONIC

When we used to go to Grandmother Morris's house, I would be assailed by the strong smell of sulfur as soon as I opened the kitchen screen door. There is nothing else that smells like sulfur, especially when your stomach is a little queasy after a long, bumpy ride.

The hand pump in Grandmother's kitchen spewed forth vile-smelling sulfur water. Papa and his brother and sisters were raised on it and would drink it with gusto. Besides the smell, it was Black sulfur. Grandmother had beautiful cut-glass drinking glasses that she would proudly set on our dinner table. I always thought they were dirty. Eventually, I realized it was not dirt but the black sulfur that concentrated in the facets of those glasses. I could not make myself drink that water.

Now my Papa, when my sister was little, used to think he was giving my sister and me a treat. He would drive for miles to where there was a sulfur spring. It would bubble in all its blackness right out of the rock. He would always bring his little tin cup and would down cup after cup of that horrible liquid. We would just watch. He would exclaim how delicious it was. Then, we would go home.

The crowning touch of sulfur was Papa's dandruff treatment. He would buy large jars of yellow sulfur powder. Then he would remove his cap and generously pour the sulfur powder into it. He would also rub it lavishly into his scalp. His once-red hair was thinning so his scalp got good coverage. Then, he would put his cap back on his head and wait for the treatment to take effect.

I don't know if the sulfur treatment made his dandruff go away. It certainly made us kids go away until the treatment wore off. And, I think it helped make the hair on the top of his head go away as it thinned quite rapidly after those treatments.

THINKING ABOUT FOOD

I have a lot of memories from Mama's kitchen. It was always hot; we couldn't afford a fan. My permanent job was to be the "fly swatter."

Mama would come in hot and tired from helping Papa in the fields or from milking, bedding and feeding the cows. She had to carry five-gallon buckets of water to those thirsty critters. They rewarded her with nods of their heads and slurpings on her arm with their long, scratchy tongues. She would have put dinner on the stove before going to the barn.

I wasn't allowed to cook much. I was allowed to stir things and turn the fried foods such as meat and fried mush and eggplant. Meat was usually fried in lard until it was black, hard and dead. There was no chance of a piece of fried meat in Mama's kitchen getting up out of the pan and running away. There was one good thing—we had lots of iron in our diet from those heavy cast-iron fry pans. When we had company, Mama would season and brown, then bake chicken in her covered fry pan. It was always tender and good because she covered it and baked it low and slow.

Sometimes, we would have cornmeal mush and milk. Papa would raise the corn. He would spend his winter evenings sitting in his rocking chair, shelling corn until his overalls were covered with red corn dust. After we had eaten cornmeal mush, we would have fried mush the next meal. We would cover it with corn syrup or fresh sorghum molasses.

I knew the molasses was fresh because I used to watch Uncle Paul press it in his sorghum cane press. After most of the juice was pressed out of the cane, the juice was cooked until it was syrupy and brown. We children got to chew the pressed cane pieces. They were our "candy."

One of Mama's favorite meals was goulash. She would put browned beef, tomato chunks, cooked macaroni and onions in a pot and let it set on low heat. Sometimes it would set so long that it was mushy. I didn't like that, but I was the only one who didn't.

We used to pick ground cherries for jam. They were what Mama called volunteers. That meant that they would come up anywhere in the garden. When they were golden yellow, we would unwrap them and eat them. It was like a little Christmas in the summer as we unwrapped our tiny presents.

Mama grew gooseberries for a while. They were okay for pie but not for much else because they were very sour. My favorite fruit pies that Mama made were elderberry cream pie and mulberry cream pie. I got to help roll out the crusts.

How I miss those days in Mama's kitchen where each dessert dish was served with lots of sugar and a double portion of love. Mama's love came from the deep joy of the Lord in her heart. I never knew the many hurts she carried deep inside. Her love from her Heavenly Father was all that showed (besides the empty plates of her well-fed family).

HAPPY THE MAN

"Trot, trot to Boston,
To buy a loaf of bread.
Trot, trot back again,
Old Trot's dead!"

I giggled as I was jounced and bounced on my old "Trot, Trot." Uncle Paul's leg endlessly trot-trotted me as he said that silly rhyme. (Some of my children remember those trot-trot rides, too.) When he was done, he would say "Skillabooch!"

Uncle Paul loved his farm, his family and his dog. He had an old barn with a low, slanted side roof, and above it was the upper wall of the barn. He had made a lake in the back fields that, he thought, resembled a dog's head. He named the lake "Dog's Head Lake." He came to me and said, "Since you are an artist, paint Dog's Head Lake for me on the barn and I'll pay you."

Now, I was very afraid of heights. However, for Uncle Paul, I was willing to do just about anything. I scrambled up on that low portion of the roof and started painting on the wall. I finished the painting—about seven feet by fifteen, with very little spilled paint. This mural, of an irregularly shaped blue lake, on the side of a barn, was by far the largest painting I ever made. There were no trees, no boats, no decorations—just a big blue blob of a lake.

*   *   *

Once Uncle Paul had a little spotted terrier named Tags. He loved that dog so much that he wanted a memorial made for him although Tags was just a mongrel. Together, they would scuffle and play tug-o-war with an old towel. Tags would follow him everywhere. One day Uncle Paul forgot to renew Tags' license. After a period of a few weeks, the dog warden came to take Tags to the pound. Uncle Paul stood his ground between the warden and his dog.

"You will not take my dog away," he growled through clenched teeth. The warden insisted that it was his job, and the dog must go.

"No, I'd sooner go to jail than allow you to take my dog away." He stood there without flinching.

"You either give up your dog or you go to jail!"

Uncle Paul went to jail. He was the only one of our family to become a jailbird. The story even made it onto the front page of the local paper, The Crescent News: "*Local Man Jailed Over Dog*," complete with a picture.

Uncle Paul truly loved life and enjoyed every moment of it. He encouraged and helped others. When he died, the Children's Choir of the Catholic Church where he worked as a janitor (although he was a Presbyterian) sang at his funeral. They sang, "Happy the Man . . . whose God is the Lord. Happy the Man . . . who knows how to pray." What a fitting tribute to a loyal, beloved, happy man whose God was the Lord.

HAY FORKS

I was my Papa's boy. He never let Mama forget that she didn't bear him a handful of strapping, strong sons. For all of my young years, I worked on the farm, doing all of the jobs any robust young boy would have done. Since we had livestock—cows, pigs and chickens, I was responsible for much of their care. I helped Papa with the hay crop that was necessary for winter cattle feed.

In mid-summer, we cut the clover field and raked the hay into windrows to dry. It would be turned over a day later. The cutting and raking process often disturbed bird and bunny nests and scattered the frightened babies. That always made me sad. Sometimes the mower blades sliced into a nest of blue racer snakes. They would wriggle and slither away in all directions.

On a sunny day, Papa would decide whether it was the day to make hay. I think he based his decision on how hot the sun was that day and how scratchy the hay had become. It always seemed there was no breeze on haymaking day. We were fortunate to have a tractor and wagon. Our neighbor had to use a pair of mules, Fred and Sadie, to pull his hay wagon.

The hay rake/conveyer was hooked behind the wagon. As we moved through the field, the rake would sweep up the windrow and elevate it to the back of the wagon. As Papa drove the tractor, it was my job on the wagon to fork the hay off the conveyer up to the front of the wagon.

Since I was afraid of heights, I always worried how I would get down off that load when it got too high. One day when the hay load was piled about as high as it could get, I was still forking. Up the conveyer came two six-foot long wriggling blue racer snakes, scooped up by the rake. It did not take me very long to figure out how to get down. One mammoth jump, and I was off and running.

When we finished loading the wagon, we took it to the barn and backed it into the center space between the haymows. At the top of the barn were two hay forks. These forks were U-shaped, about three feet across with pointed ends. They were fastened to ropes that ran from a pulley on a track across the top of the barn. At a signal, a rope would loosen and allow the forks to drop onto that load of hay. Then the forks closed with their load and were hoisted to the top of the barn. The load moved along the track until it was released into the haymow. It was dangerous to be the one in the mow pulling the rope to drop the load.

One summer day I knew there were new kittens in the haymow. Papa was ready to drop the load.

"Papa, No!" I screamed. "Let me get the kittens first!"

He didn't pay any attention. I scrambled up the ladder to pull the kittens to safety, but I was too late. The load dropped. I was sad for three days for those poor squashed babies. Sad, until one day I heard little "mew-mew's" coming from the other side of the haymow. Mama cat had saved her babies. They were safe until the next cutting of hay.

AUNTIE

She was sturdy but frail, strict but sentimental—my dear old Auntie. Aunt Edna had the most pronounced widow's hump I have ever seen on a vertical person. She was thin and wrinkled, not at all like some of the other buxom ladies of her family. She had never married and lived alone in a small white frame house a half-mile down the road from us.

At her house I made the transition from a little girl to a young woman. I remember sleeping on her old couch until I could no longer fit. I later found out that it was a half-size antique walnut Victorian Rococo bed. Who could have known what was there under that pile of homemade comforters and quilts, many of them made by Auntie.

My Mama pronounced Aunt Edna the most socialized, the most prestigious and closest to nobility of the whole Myers clan. Auntie had been the housekeeper for poet Edgar A. Guest in Detroit for a number of years. From all of those years in his presence, his esthetic nature rubbed off on her and transferred down to Mama and me.

Aunt Edna was the one who first taught me the wonders of oil painting. Under her tutelage I painted my first oil painting which won first prize in the Defiance County Fair—probably because it was the only entry in my age category. I remember her cigar box of old squashed and pressed tubes of oil paints. She gave them to me when she could no longer see to paint. Some were hard and dry, not good for painting. I kept them in a safe place for years because they were a gift from her. I also have her first painting, a moon-lit scene of a sail boat in a bay, painted on a cheese box lid. To this very day, the smell of oil paint excites me and evokes her memory.

I never received any other mementos from Auntie. I wanted that pair of Pilgrim dolls she had and kept hinting that she should give them to me. They were about five inches tall, made of porcelain and clothed in stiff crepe paper Pilgrim outfits. I knew where she hid them in the china cabinet. But one day, they were missing. Did she give them to someone else? How could she think they would be treasured as much by anyone else but me? I preferred to assume that they were stolen.

Auntie tended the most beautiful flowerbeds imaginable. Her little house was surrounded in every nook and cranny by ferns and flowers. Old-fashioned ones like pink and white spirea, hollyhocks, althea and mallows. I used to pretend the spirea petals were snowflakes raining down from heaven. Foxgloves and bleeding hearts peeked out from under trees. Red and pink Dianthus gathered in clumps around the front porch. Her lilies, dozens of kinds, filled the backyard with fragrance, competing with the roses which were antique varieties passed down from earlier generations of Myers and Schuberts. I, as a little girl, exclaimed in awe, "Some day I will have my own old-fashioned flower garden like Auntie's."

Later memories of Auntie, before she was weakened by cancer and took to her bed, were of the wonderful aromas coming from her kitchen. Sour cream pie, creamed elderberry pie, sour cherry pie all were served in blue graniteware pie pans. Her specialty was cooked caraway-seed cheese. I remember her, in her long chintz apron, her thin, strong hands chopping hard cheeses into her little cooking pot, adding cream, caraway seeds and some mysterious ingredients. She would cook this tasty cheese and let it rest a day before serving it. The thought of it brings back a rush of memories. I have yet to find that caraway cheese recipe—it must have been an original.

HENRIETTA

One day Mama came to me and said, "I have something I want you to have and then to give to your little girl." She carefully produced something wrapped in soft yellow fringed fabric. She gently unwrapped it and told me this story:

"When I was a little girl, about six or so, I got very sick. They called it 'intermittent fever'. Your Grandma Myers thought that I would die. She wanted to give me a few happy moments while I was still alive. Then she gave me this old dolly that had been made in the Old Country (Germany). I named her Henrietta. Grandma said I was not to show her to anyone." That would be vanity—a sign of pride.

"Oh, but I was proud! I so much wanted my friends to see that I had something new and pretty. I took my dolly and held her up at the window so that my friends passing by could see her."

"Well, Grandma found out, and was she unhappy! Because of that, sick as I was, she took my dolly away. There would be NO proud people in Our house! I did not see Henrietta for many, many years. Now, you care for her just as I wanted to do, and pass her on to your little girl."

COWPOKE

Although we did not have a large herd of milk cows, it was my job to retrieve the cows for milking each evening. In the winter, we kept the cows in the barnyard during the day. The barnyard became a brown, soupy, mucky, stinky mess. When we brought them into the barn, they still smelled of the yard, and we soon did, too. I preferred the summer when I was at home and had to get the cows from pasture. "Pasture" meant a half-mile walk down the lane to the woods where the cows somehow found good things to eat.

The walk down the lane was always enjoyable. I had a tendency to dawdle because there were so many things to examine—the milkweed pods bursting into tiny stars of cotton in the fall, the purple asters with golden centers, tiny mushroom buttons popping up out of the moist soil. I would pick sprays of goldenrod and purple asters for my Mama and add the airy Queen Anne's lace to the bouquet. I loved to smell the lavender Monardia, growing wild, that had a minty scent and looked like tiny skyrockets shooting off their stems. Then there were the mud puddles . . . I had to poke them with a stick to see what creatures lived there, earthworms, wigglers, crickets, tadpoles and flying grasshoppers.

The best part of the walk was seeing the "Trees of Heaven." That's what I called the two large elm trees that guarded the gate to the woods pasture. They were so tall and grand. I always thought that trees like those would guard heaven's portal. I was ready to enter in.

After I unlocked the gate, I would try to round up the cows. The rest of the woods was not heavenly. There were brambles, holes to fall into and spider webs that got tangled in my face and hair. I also had to watch out for snakes that lolled by the little stream in the woods. When I finally found all of the cows, we would start back.

The cows, despite their comical appearance, are not dumb creatures. They are very intelligent and can be extremely deceptive and unpredictable. I would think I had the herd all together; then one of them would bolt and run the other direction.

I was very hot and tired one day when I went to get the cows for milking. Since I did not have a horse to ride to round up the herd, I thought perhaps I could ride a cow up the long lane to the barn. I selected Molly, a young heifer who was one of my favorites. I moved that little cow over against the fence and tried to climb onto her from the top of the fence. I slid right over her to the ground on the other side. I tried again with the same results. It was then that I realized cows' backs are round and slippery and not built for riding. After several more tries, with the heifer becoming more and more agitated, I was on her back.

"Ouch, that hurt!" I learned that cows do not come with a built-in saddle. Where her back should go down for my comfort, her spine went up. Molly wriggled and I squirmed. I was afraid of hurting her. She seemed more fragile than ever before. My tailbone hurt, so I slid off as gracefully as I could. Molly never told anyone about my clumsy attempt to be a cow rider. It was then that I vowed I would never again be a cowpoke—because the cow poked me!

THE STORY MACHINE

Here it is! How wonderful! I have looked for it so long. It is torn and fragile and falling apart. But I found it! It used to be stored in the attic of the concrete block house for many years after we moved into the big house. But here it is, in Papa's basement amid piles of rubbish and papers. Mama had saved it and carefully wrapped it in brown paper and tied it with a string, as though she knew how much it meant to me—the Bible Story Machine.

When I was young, we lived for at least sixteen years in the three-room square block house which was damp, chilly and often moldy. It was to be temporary until Papa could build our big house. It was concrete block on the outside with lath and plaster on the inside, even the ceilings. When weather was wet, the ceilings would swell. Sometimes the lath strips would break, and the ceilings would crack or break loose, showering everything with plaster and dust.

In my childhood, we were the last family in Highland Township to have electricity. When my friends were entertaining their friends, they showed off their new radios. I thought how wonderful it would be to have a radio, a refrigerator and maybe some day one of those boxes that showed moving pictures of people. They all used electricity. I couldn't imagine how something like an electric moving picture box would work.

When my friends did come over (which was very rare), I had to entertain with what we had—the Bible Story Machine. It was a long strip of paper, maybe twenty-five feet long and about a foot wide, that rolled from one cylinder to another, like in between two scrolls, telling the Bible story. It was very dramatically illustrated with majestic figures like Moses, with his hand upraised, leading the people. I believe there was a battery-operated sound box at one time to add to the special effects. Although it didn't compare to a radio, it was all we had.

One day, one of my friends, whom I wanted very much to impress, came for a visit along with her parents. I was embarrassed by our house, our poor possessions, the cracked and bulging ceiling. While the big folks talked in the living room, I proudly (and bravely) showed off the picture machine at our kitchen table. We had just had a rainy season; the ceiling overhead was bulging farther than ever. When we came to the most exciting part of the whole story—the ceiling fell—tearing the final picture in half just like the veil of the temple being torn apart in the real story of Jesus.

MY SPECIAL HORSE

I think some time in every farm girl's life, she wants a horse for her very own. I was one of those farm girls. I desperately wanted a horse. Maybe it was because I wanted a friend so badly. I figured a horse would be a loyal friend who didn't tell secrets. Besides that, my friend would take me to wonderful places. We could dream of magical places together.

"Papa, Papa, may I please have a horse? I pleaded. I asked him several times. Usually he was silent. Finally, one day my Papa answered my plea.

"We cannot have a horse on our farm," he said.

"But why?" I asked.

"Because I am very allergic to horses. Whenever I am around them, I break out in hives and get very sick," was his reply.

"Oh," I thought. "I would never want to have anything or do anything that would hurt my papa."

So I passed the days, dreaming of a horse but knowing it was not possible.

Beside our barn stood the old corn crib. Its unpainted, slotted sides allowed the wind to blow through freely, making soft, moaning sounds. Mounds of corncobs were reminders of harvest's gold. I felt an air of mystery there. Along the back wall was a horizontal wooden beam that braced the sides of the crib. Upon examination, I found a notch carved out about sixteen inches long and three inches deep along the top of the beam. Just the right size for a saddle. I placed a large stepping stone beneath it, scrambled onto the beam and settled into the notch. I tried my new "horse," and it fit just fine. Splinters along the sides scratched my legs, but I hardly noticed. I had found my horse.

I spent many happy hours in the saddle. Sometimes he was a gleaming palomino or a shining black stallion. We rode together to rescue someone in distress through fields ablaze with wild daisies. We would jump fences and chase the wind. Other times I was the fair maiden in distress on a brown pony who was rescued by a dashing knight on a magnificent white stallion. We rode side by side across the moat and into the castle.

Years flew by. I rode that old horse until I went to college. I grew up, married and had a life of my own. Then one day Mama died. It was a sad occasion knowing Papa must survive without her. Papa died several years later.

As I was talking to relatives and friends gathered at Papa's viewing, one old fellow spoke to me. He said he used to be one of my Papa's best friends when they were young. I asked him about some of the things they did when they were young men. He replied, "Well, your father . . . He was one of the best horse trainers in the county."

As for the corn crib . . . The home place traded hands many times. The old corn crib leans precariously, the wind still whistling through its sides. And there, along the back wall, hidden in the shadows, my loyal horse still waits for me.

THE OUTHOUSE

Slosh, slosh, slosh. My slippers slogged through the wet snow. The icy rain stung my cheeks and coated my lashes. Morning light was bursting through the branches of Papa's apple tree. I fumbled with the latch, feeling fortunate that I didn't have to wait in line. Once inside, it was dry and roomy. It was a two-seater although I didn't want to share. And, we had real toilet paper, not the Sears Roebuck catalog like some of our neighbors did. The seats were of dark, smooth, polished hardwood. After all, Papa was a carpenter by trade. He put the roof and the sides on our outhouse. He didn't pour the cement base; he bought it somewhere. It had an emblem with "King" written on it, centered right under the wooden seats. There was a little window up high to provide light and to prevent peepers. There was no moon cutout on the door so it looked more like a regular little house.

When I was little, and lived in the block house, we used a chamber pot. Mama didn't want the rest of us to have to go outside in the cold so she took care of it. I have seen some very pretty, floral decorated pots, but we could only afford a plain one. We were glad for the outhouse when it was finished, for Mama's sake and ours, too. In good weather, the path wound through Mama's flower beds and under the pretty willow tree. If I chose to tarry, I could watch the bees feeding on her peonies.

Every child should be allowed to visit a quality outhouse like ours. After all, we sat in royalty because it was a "King."

PAPA'S BASEMENT

I was on the way to Papa's basement to fetch a jar of peaches. It was Papa's basement because it had mostly his stuff in it. I tried to tell Mama I didn't want to go down there, but she insisted. She did not realize that I feared the black monster who lived in the dark coal bin behind the furnace. My terror was real. The light switch to the furnace room was broken, and I had to go through that room to get to the canned goods room.

I carefully descended the crumbling cement steps to the basement. Dank, musty odors smacked me in the face as I stepped onto the wet concrete floor. To my left was the vegetable storage room. Odors from rotting carrots, spoiling turnips and apples filled the air with mold and made me sneeze. Mice had spilled a bushel of walnuts stored there and carried them into the other rooms.

To my right was Mama's wash room. It was a gloomy room with low ceilings strung with clothes lines. She would hang her wash on these lines in the winter. The clothes never smelled fresh like outdoors. The two dingy windows were never opened because vines and weeds had intertwined with the opening levers. Planks were on the floor for us to walk on because the basement often flooded.

I hurried on, my shoes soaking wet from the water that squished up through holes in the planks. It rained a week ago, and water had poured through a broken window at ground level, filling the room ahead of me with a half-inch of water. Walnuts floated on the murky water. Soggy newspapers broke free from their cords and lay in moldy heaps.

Ahead was the dark cavern of the furnace room. Cobwebs from the rough open beams tangled my hair and stuck to my lashes. In the darkness, I sprang from board to board. Suddenly, the coal furnace gave a hideous groan. The Monster . . . behind it . . . in the coal bin! Prickles and cold sweat ran down my spine. I screamed and pushed through cobwebs, brushing aside strings of dirty twine hanging from the wall and nearly falling on a rusty shovel.

I made it to the canned goods room and flooded it with light from its one hanging bulb. The vinegar barrel stood in the corner, its pungent odor permeating the air. I rocked it, noting that it was almost full. Brushing aside the dust, I grabbed a jar, switched off the light and sprinted for the stairway. I rushed past the concrete stairwell where we were supposed to hide from a tornado. I'd rather face the tornado than spend more time in Papa's basement.

I was quite proud of my courage and boldness in escaping the Monster as I handed the jar to Mama. She frowned, "But, why did you bring me tomatoes?"

AUNT TILLIE

The first glance made people turn away. She was horribly disfigured, deformed, blemished. From her flesh great and small nodules hung, making her thin frame look more fragile. The disease had ravaged her. Elephantiasis had destroyed her eyesight, her hearing and even her flesh itself. What untold misery this poor woman had suffered. Yet disease could not destroy her spirit—or her soul. Caroline Mathilde Martch could not be put down easily. She had learned to rest her soul on a Rock and to place her body in the hands of the Great Physician.

Elephantiasis is a disease caused by infection of minute parasitic worms which, in turn, causes enlargement and thickening of the tissues. It can be horribly disfiguring. Aunt Tillie Martch suffered almost all of its devastating effects. The disease, followed by a fever, attacked her as a young woman and struck her down, taking away her beauty and vitality.

Aunt Tillie and her brother, Johann Peter Martch (Uncle Pete) lived on the farm north of us. They worked the Martch homestead land year after year, raising chickens, corn, wheat, beans and oats.

Uncle Pete appeared to be stern, foreboding and brooding. He would tramp through the house with his big boots covered with barn dirt and dried manure. Barn odors clung to his clothes and made his heavy beard smell foul. He and Tillie scrimped and saved. There were no frills at their house, not even electricity but his sister never complained. Amazingly, Pete died quite a wealthy man.

After Pete's death, Aunt Tillie's health declined until she was unable to keep her own home. She was transferred to a nursing home. She could neither see nor hear. Yet, she would sing songs to Jesus in her cracked, scratchy voice. She would sit and crochet the most beautiful doilies and edged handkerchiefs. I do not understand how she could choose such pretty colors or do such intricate stitches when her eyesight had gone.

She was an example of sincere devotion to God such as I have rarely seen anywhere. It was a joy to visit the nursing home, to walk down the hall toward the last door on the left where I would hear that sweet, scratchy voice singing, "Oh, How I Love Jesus." I believe in heaven her voice and her body were made perfect to sing praise to her Jesus.

LOVE FEASTING

I scooted across the rough plank bench, making room for Mama and Papa. I bit my lip as splinters ripped through my new skirt into my leg. I was nine years old and it hurt enough to make me cry. We were at the table at the Dunkard Love Feast. Papa had been excited about this all summer, and now we were here. We wakened at four o'clock that Sunday morning, milked the cows, put on our best church clothes, and traveled to North Creek, Ohio, where the festivity was held.

Papa's family were Dunkards, a conservative, pacificistic branch of the Old Order Brethren Church. They were sometimes called Dunkers or Tunkers because they believed in immersion baptism by dunking three times, once for the Father, once for the Son and once for the Holy Spirit. The members wore plain clothing, men with beards, hats and standing collars on their black coats. Women like my Aunt Rebecca wore plain dark bonnets and hoods. I remember seeing her bustling about in her hot kitchen, cooking, in her heavy, long dress with its wool cape. She always wore her head covering even though heat from the wood range made rivulets of sweat run down her face.

We arrived at the farm where the feast was held at about nine o'clock. The men sat on one side of the big meeting room and the women and children on the other. The service began with singing of hymns. There were no musical instruments but the combined voices were rich and melodious. Then came the sermons. Several men would speak or sing as the Spirit moved them. Although there were many periods of silence during the four-hour service, every man was expected to participate. The benches were very hard, and I found it difficult to remember what they were saying.

At one o'clock we gathered for the Love Feast. Since Papa was not a member, we were allowed at the Feast but not for the Eucharist and Foot Washing that followed. The congregation was seated by families on wooden benches under the trees behind makeshift twelve-foot plank tables supported by saw horses. Baskets of fresh, homemade bread sat in front of us, but there was no butter or jam. Each person had a large porridge bowl. A piping hot bowl of broth and with chunks of boiled beef was placed in front of us. The aroma was heavenly. We broke off pieces of bread and dunked it into the common bowl of broth. Papa spooned out a hunk of fatty beef for me. I nearly gagged when I saw all of that boiled fat. I was expected to clean my bowl and waste nothing. I felt sick and somehow managed to escape eating all of my meat. There were thanksgiving prayers, then all was quiet except the slurping of the Dunkards as they ate.

I was quite sure these people were called Dunkards because they dunked their bread into the broth. It was not until much later that I learned the real reason they were called Dunkards. As we returned home, I thought about those plain, devout people, and I admired them because they clung to their customs, traditions and beliefs in the midst of a changing and materialistic society.

OUR GREAT TRIP

Mama always wanted to travel away from our northwestern corner of Ohio to see wonderful and magnificent sights. That was her dream until she died. I inherited this wanderlust from her. Her relatives: Aunt Edna (Auntie), told her of the wonders of Detroit where she had worked and of Cleveland, the "big city". Uncle Harmon told how marvelous the Grand Canyon was and brought her a piece of petrified wood. She always treasured it. Another uncle had been "down south" to Texas. Uncle Paul filled her head with the most intriguing stories of when he was a Great Lakes ship captain. What adventurous tales he brought from those rough, tough sailors.

Mama didn't have to travel around the world. She just wanted to go SOMEWHERE.

Each summer she would ask Papa if we could go on a little vacation. Papa always said "No"—he had too much work to do, or we could not afford such frivolousness. Mama cried a bit. She wanted us kids to have something to tell our classmates when we had to write "What I Did On My Summer Vacation". Every year we had to write and read our essays on that topic.

One summer, I suppose Papa got tired of Mama's begging and agreed to spend two days for traveling. That meant we would stay overnight somewhere new. I had never stayed anywhere except at my aunt's house. I was so excited!

We left home at 4:00 a.m. and headed south. Where were we going? We didn't know, just south. It was an adventure! At this point I had only been out of the State of Ohio over the state line into Michigan to visit my cousins. Mama wanted to see where her cousin, Blake, lived in Bowling Green, Ohio, just forty miles away. It was too early to waken him so we drove by.

Then we drove and drove. I had never been in the car for that long before. Mama wanted to see the Blue Hole in Castalia and the Serpent Mound. Her Indian blood was showing. I thought the mound wasn't much to see.

Then came the Big Event! We crossed the Ohio River into Kentucky. Now I had been in two states besides Ohio. We found a rooming house and stayed overnight on the Kentucky side.

First thing in the morning, Papa wanted to get going. He had work to do. So, we headed home—not stopping for anything. I was happy. At least I had something to write about for my summer vacation!

PLAYING ON THE BACK SEAT

Aileen and I sat playing jacks on the back seat of the grange hall. When we would reach for the ball, sometimes we'd get nasty splinters from the rough boards.

Papa and Mama were members of the Grange, a farmers' organization similar to the Farm Bureau, that provided benefits to the farmers who joined. Our Grange was a secret organization whose members met once a month in the Highland Township building in our Northwestern Ohio neighborhood. My papa was often elected the Master of the local Grange. He was then responsible for chairing the meetings and assembling the regalia used in the ceremonies. He would get out ceremony books and a gavel and lay out velvet scarves commemorating ceremonial positions in the hall. He gave each officer a staff to hold and a velvet blue sash with gold tassels covered with Grange symbols which they wore diagonally from shoulder to side.

The Grange hall was a drafty wooden frame building with shabby unpainted hardwood floors and almost undecorated dirty tan walls. Drab green curtains hung over the windows that were washed maybe once a year. There were a couple mellowed, water-stained pictures of farm scenes on opposing walls. There were benches around the sides, leaving the center of the hall open. It was either too hot or too cold inside, and always smelled musty when Papa opened the door. A creaky old out-of-tune piano sat in the left front corner. The sustain pedal squeaked, and the d's and e's sometimes would not play. A cantankerous pot-belly woodstove sat in the center back and was famous for belching out more black smoke than heat. The curtains and benches collected the smoke as it filtered down in chunks.

When grangers met, there was always "The Ceremony." My friend Aileen and I had to sit in the back and be quiet. We were supposed to sit on the splintery, hard floor and write our homework papers on those rough wooden benches.

When Mama would play "The Russian Imperial March," the Grange officers would march. With staffs in hand, they would circle the hall, stopping and stomping their staffs at the stations of Ceres, Pomona and Flora. Ceres was the Roman goddess of grain, Pomona the goddess of fruit, and Flora was the goddess of flowers. The only lines of the ceremony I remember were from the Bible, "Weeping may endure for a night, but joy cometh in the morning." The rest of the ceremony and the business session was very long and boring for us children. When I got older, I was given the honor of being the assistant piano player. That made the sessions more tolerable.

Aileen and I used to play after the business meeting while the grown folks socialized. I wanted desperately for her to be my real friend. But, she lived in a large, modern house painted sparkling white. I lived in our unpainted cement block building with no running water. She had new, store-bought clothes abounding with ribbons and lace. I wore well-used Mama-made clothes that had seen many washings. We were friends at the Grange because I was the only other girl around for her.

As we giggled together about the old folks, we hid behind the benches in the back and copied how the older people walked and talked. Then one day I got brave. I pretended I was crippled, all stooped over like Old Jake Sponser, and I hobbled with a cane. I did this right in front of him. I will never forget what Old Jake said when he saw me imitating him. He straightened himself the best he could, pointed his cane at me and in his gruff voice said, "Young lady, if you make fun of someone, you will end up just like him." I never forgot his solemn warning, especially when my arthritis acts up and my back hurts.

COOKING FOR THRESHERS

My Mama was a good cook. Everyone said so. We kids thought so too. When she was in her kitchen, she "cooked for threshers." Her table was bountiful. There was always plenty for everyone, even unexpected visitors.

When I was little, Mama believed the old adage "a fat child is a healthy child". In the old German tradition, the child must be plump with rosy cheeks. She always wanted me to be healthy—and she succeeded.

Sometimes we were downright poor when the crops weren't good or equipment had broken parts to be replaced. When we were really out of money, I remember her "frog soup". It had no relation to live frogs in the water. She would roll balls of flour and lard, fry them until browned, add salt, water or milk and serve. Ukkk! And poor Mama, she tried so hard.

We always planted a garden. My Papa's gardens over the years were the most beautiful and productive in the whole neighborhood. We raised lots of things besides the traditional beans and tomatoes. We had parsnips, salsify (which Mama called the vegetable oyster), turnips, rutabagas and kohlrabi (double ukkk!). My Uncle Paul taught us to raise and eat sugar beets.

Mama canned everything she could get her hands on. In her little canned goods cellar I remember seeing jars of plums, cherries, peaches and pears. There were rows and rows of tomatoes, green beans, peas and pumpkin. She canned sausages, chicken chunks and hunks of beef that I really liked. Mama even canned grapes and elderberries—to make juice, jam and jelly. Her canned strawberries tasted much better as jam so I was glad when she had time to make it.

There were a couple desserts I didn't like—like big pearl tapioca not made with the juicy, sweet white sauce. I'd try to choke it down but it looked like bleached eyeballs. I never did let Papa know I like tapioca, no matter who cooks it. I didn't really like Mama's square pan sugar cookies because I saw how much lard she put in them. Lard came from those butchered pigs, the poor things.

Mama could make some wonderful, wonderful pies and cakes. My sister and I thought they were the best. She used her fresh peaches, rhubarb, apples and cherries. I used to help her. Mama let me make my own little brown sugar pies in tiny little metal pans. She could make creamed elderberry pies that would make our mouths water. And, green tomato pie—that was a real treat. I fondly remember her baked cheese pies. How I wish I could find her recipes for them. They were so-o-o good.

Harvest time came and Mama outdid herself. Papa had rounded up neighborhood men who came to help thresh the wheat and oats. The threshers used the old horse-pulled threshing machines. They had noisy engines that belched smoke and dust all over the men.

Mama put out her spread in the dining room. The men came in, all hot, dusty and sweaty. Dirty or not, she treated them like royalty with her best linen tablecloth covering the table. Then she brought out steaming mashed potatoes and gravy, fried chicken and stuffing, roast beef, too. She'd make creamed corn from her own home-dried corn, stewed tomatoes, baked beans and cold slaw. There was lots of lemonade to drink. Then for dessert, she would have cookies, a cake or two and a couple of pies.

The men were stuffed until they could hardly move, let alone go out and work in the hot sun. I looked forward to those meals but not to the thought of all of those dishes to wash. I was the official and only dishwasher.

Those times have passed. The old home place no longer hosts threshers, butchers and hay-makers. Every once in a while I get a hankering for Mama's cooking. Just for the chance to see her again, I'd even eat a bowl of pearl tapioca.

AT CHRISTMAS TIME

Christmas time down on the farm with Mama and Papa seems so far away in time. Almost like it never happened. Yet, there are memories to tell.

We would prepare for Christmas the night before. Mama would pop popcorn. What we didn't eat, we would string on long threads and wind around the tree. The tree was always the one from the attic, with fold-out branches, dusty and quite worn as years passed. Although on the "other place" as we called Mama's home place, there were a lot of evergreens growing, we never thought of cutting one. We always stored our tree in the attic of the concrete block house. After the popcorn, we strung chains of cranberries. There were old glass ornaments with the paint flaking off and little hand-made trinkets my sister and I brought home from school.

Papa would always read the Christmas Story out of the Sunday School lesson booklet on Christmas Eve. Then we would pray—for all the relatives, the poor, and those who had strayed from God's path. It was always the same prayer. I used to wonder if God got tired of hearing the same thing.

After devotions, Mama would bring set out our wrapping paper from the old wooden cheese box from the attic. We wrapped our little gifts and placed them under the tree. It was amazing on Christmas morning how those few gifts multiplied. We never talked about Santa Claus, but my friends told me he did it.

When Christmas Day dawned, Mama had already been up working. She always cooked more food than we needed. Aunt Betty would come, and Uncle George (Papa's brother), in the years before he died of cancer. Other dear people would drop in but not for the meal, Mama's brother and his family, Aunt Stella and her children, Papa's friends, Mama's best friend, Ruth, sometimes her Myers cousins and often the Pastor. Mama would do herself proud in the kitchen. Although others offered to bring food, Mama would do most of the work, and we girls would help. Mama's best linen tablecloth covered the table which was set with her green pressed-glass dinnerware and real silverware. It was my job to polish it the week before, as well as her silver gravy pitcher and ladle. I remember her green and yellow daffodil glasses which she would fill with Koolaid. Christmas Dinner would include: her mashed potatoes piled high, usually candied sweet potatoes, green beans, baked chicken so tender it dripped off the bones, and roast beef with gravy. There was always her cranberry salad, dried corn, then pies, and two kinds of cakes topped off with whipped cream—the real kind. We kids nibbled Mama's sugar cookies while we waited for the meal to begin.

All of our family members would look forward to the little box Mama gave each of us. We would carefully open the box, then rush to hide it so no one would find it. Inside the box was total decadence—Mama's homemade chocolate fudge with hand-picked hickory nuts or walnuts, homemade peanut brittle, creamy penuche, and the best pink and white divinity fudge you ever licked of your fingers.

After we were properly stuffed, the women folks would go to the kitchen to wash dishes, and the men would retire to the living room to discuss the weather, the local gossip and the price of soybeans while they chewed on pieces of hard ribbon candy.

Papa liked to recite readings from his Grange drama book. Then he would get out his fiddle and squeak through "She'll Be Comin' Around the Mountain," "Turkey in the Straw" and "Twinkle, Twinkle Little Star." He only played for us after Christmas and Easter Dinners. Following the concert, we'd gather around the Chinese checker board for a couple hours.

By this time, we were so tired and lazy that we were ready to be tucked into our beds—and dream of another happy Christmas.

PAPA'S APPLES

Papa owned an apple orchard which was back behind the chicken house. He also raised delicious pears, peaches and plums. He was almost daily in his orchard, pruning, spraying and just watching his trees.

One day as he was going to the orchard, he said, "Rachel, I want you to go with me. I want to teach you about grafting and budding fruit trees."

He was carrying a sharp knife, tape, screwdriver, chisel and some gooey stuff I later learned was grafting compound. "Here, carry these," he said.

"What do you mean, 'grafting and budding'?" I was pleased that he wanted me to accompany him, but I didn't know anything about caring for trees.

Papa explained, "Grafting means that you insert a stem with leaf buds into the original part of the tree trunk. The upper part of the graft, called the scion, becomes the top of the tree whereas the root and trunk is called the stock. The apples we want will come from the top part of the tree."

"But, why do you want to do that?" I questioned.

"Some trees and vines do not become a true tree from their seeds. They revert back to a wild plant. If we graft, we will reproduce a tree like the tree from which the graft stalk is taken. For example, we can graft a Red Delicious onto a wild apple root stock, and the tree will yield Red Delicious apples."

I was awed by this information but had a lot of questions like "What trees or plants can be grafted?" and "How do you do it?" and "What is budding?"

Papa showed me a young tree. He said that trees up to five years old are best for grafting. Most varieties of a fruit species can be grafted to each other including those of a different variety. He showed me a Red Delicious apple grafted onto a Yellow Delicious tree. The tree would produce two kinds of apples. He also said that you cannot graft or bud trees of different species that have different seeds together. (I tried it and he was right!) Usually he would graft his trees in April or May before blossom time. Then he showed me methods of grafting like the Whip Graft and the Cleft Graft. He showed me how to place a single bud (Budding) into the stock tree instead of a section of stem. He bound the grafts together tightly and covered them with gooey grafting compound.

"Now, all we have to do is wait," he said, "and let Nature take its course."

For two years we waited until those grafts and budded branches produced fruit. Papa had many varieties of apples such as: Red Delicious, Jonathan, Grimes Golden, MacIntosh, Northern Spy and Baldwin. I knew he had obtained fresh scions from his friends or neighbors for many of these. He also had friends at Defiance College agriculture classes who swapped scions with him. Then, one day I helped Papa place his little sign in the front lawn, "Apples For Sale." The customers came for miles to buy our delicious apples. No one appreciated those apples more than I did as I munched a tasty ripe Jonathan.

MELON HEAD

As I became a teenager, I began to sing in the youth choir of our church. I started singing around the eighth grade when the Ringenbergs pastured our church. There were many older teens in the choir, and I admired their voices and character. I respected one girl so much that I decided to go to whatever college she chose because I thought she had so much wisdom.

Our next pastor's wife led our choir and used to drive out into the country to pick up the teens who had no ride for practice. I was one of them. Usually there were five or six girls in the car plus the driver. We traveled over a lot of dusty, dirt roads to get back to the church for choir practice.

My Uncle George, who died in the mid-fifties, lived in a tiny house next to the church. He was a bachelor, and Mama was concerned that perhaps he wasn't eating right. He was ill with cancer. Mama would gather a large bag of foodstuffs for him each week: cookies, breads, custards and garden produce. It was my job to deliver the food to him after choir practice.

I remember the evening Mama sent a lovely cantaloupe to Uncle George. Since the car was crowded, I held the food and the cantaloupe tightly on my lap. I was in the center of the back seat. There were six of us girls squashed into that car.

We were traveling down a gravel road pretty fast. When Mrs. Pastor realized we were going too fast, she thought she was pressing down on the brake. Instead, she put her foot on the gas hard. We started fishtailing faster and faster. I knew we were going to crash. I clutched the melon tightly and prayed desperately, "Jesus, help us!"

The car started to roll over. The side front door flew open. I kept my eyes open and stayed on the bottom, watching the other girls fly over me. My cousin, Joyce, flew out of the car. As the car flipped, it would have landed on Joyce except that it landed on the edge of the open door and bounced over her. God protected all of us, and we only had bumps and cuts. But, that beautiful melon was totally smashed. I felt so sorry I couldn't give it to Uncle George.

OUR WALL PHONE

"R-i-n-n-g" after three turns of the crank, I heard
"Hell-o-o-o." Olive Deepee's friendly voice clattered in my ear.
"Hello Central, I want to speak with my cousin Ruth."
"Oka-a-y," she plugged my phone line into Ruth's.

I had to stand up to talk into our wall phone because I was too short. I loved that old phone because, through its hand-held receiver and mouthpiece, I could call my friends and relatives even though they lived far away and even called a boyfriend in later years.

Since we lived in a small rural community, we had party lines. Everyone knew everyone else, and Olive Deepee knew everybody. She probably knew everyone's deepest secrets because she could hear what all of us said. With a party line, each family had a different ring. Ours was two long rings. Mr. Brakebill, across the road, had one long ring. Some folks had short rings or a combination of longs and shorts. If there was a community emergency, there were four long rings, and everyone ran to their phones.

During a thunder storm with plenty of lightning, we all stayed far from the phone. I remember one time Mama held me close when the phone rang during a storm. Fire shot from the mouthpiece of the wall phone ten feet across the room. Anyone who answered the phone would certainly get an earfull.

One day we visited the local phone office where Olive Deepee worked. She sat in a little booth-like room with one window, surrounded by high boards full of holes. She wore earphones. When someone would call, she would pick up a cord with a plug on the end and put the plug into one of the holes. Once in a while she would put the plug in the wrong hole, and the caller would get a surprise when the phone was answered.

I loved our old worn wall phone with polish and grime rubbed into its surface. I spent many happy moments talking there. After I grew older and returned to the home place, I noticed the wall phone had been replaced by a desk phone with rotary dial. I found out that Olive Deepee had been replaced by electronic circuitry. In Papa's basement I found the discarded old wall phone and toted it to my own home. Each time I see it, I relive favorite old memories at our wall phone.

MOVING DAY

Papa was a carpenter. For many years while we lived in the little cement block house, he talked of building a large, modern house for us. This talk went on from when I was born until the end of my eleventh year of high school. Perhaps after a time, he was tired of doing large carpentry projects since he had been the supervisor of the building of our local school. Anyway, he decided to take a short cut.

One day he took us for a ride to the little burg of New Bavaria, about seven miles away. There he pointed out a two-story house that was for sale. He liked it. We really weren't excited about the house because it was nothing special. Papa bought it and made preparations to move it to our property.

Such a move, in the fifties, was unheard of in our area. Power lines had to be cut. A special flat bed trailer to carry the house had to be built. The trip was mapped out and involved five extra miles of travel because some of the roads were too narrow or the curves too tight.

.Moving day came and the house, which had been set up on blocks, was loaded onto the trailer. Neighbors watched from behind curtained windows. Imagine! A house going down the road! Some old-timers said it couldn't be done, that the trailer would break down or the house would fall off. Papa was determined to complete the move. He walked the whole distance beside his house.

Although the move was successful, a sad thing happened. During his walk, Papa stepped into a hole beside the road and seriously sprained his back and hip. In great pain, he completed the trip and got the house settled on the concrete basement he had built. After getting the necessary electricity and water and heating pipes in place, Papa lost interest in the project. Perhaps the pain caused it, but Papa never finished the inside of his house, preferring to lie on the sofa as Mama and I tended the animals and garden. He was never the same again.

SAUSAGE STUFFING

When we butchered, it was a BIG event. Some of the relatives would come and help. Papa was proud of his fat pigs. One of them was my friend, Pork-a-Line. I used to feed her six-foot hogweeds and ragweeds from the garden. It was hard to see her be butchered because it was my job to feed her every day.

We prepared and ate every part of the pig that was edible. When it came to head cheese which was scraps and leftovers cooked in a gel, I knew for sure it was not edible. I would get my seat tanned royally if I didn't sit at the table and eat every bite. The same went for brains, pickled pig feet, souse, stomach and kidneys. My little tummy rebelled at the gristle chunks in the souse. I wasn't sure God intended for every part of the animal to be eaten. As time passed, I learned to eat heart, tongue and liver and even to cook them properly.

The pig's stomach and intestines were cleaned out and washed in preparation for making sausage. I got to help turn the handle of the sausage stuffer. On butchering day, we kids got cracklings (fried fat after the lard was rendered out) for a treat.

Then, Mama would take all the big chunks of meat, especially the loin, hams and shoulders and cuts for bacon and spread them out on a big oil-cloth covered table. She would liberally douse them with Morton's Salt Cure, rubbing it in until every surface was covered. The meat would then be stored for several weeks until cured. At the holidays, a roasted pork loin was about as good a treat as we could imagine.

AUNT BETTY'S HOUSE

My Aunt Elizabeth (Aunt Betty) was a regal gal. Whenever I think of her, I think of Great Britain's Queen Elizabeth. She was of almost royal lineage. She had a German prince in her ancestry. Part of it was the way she carried herself, tall, straight and with honor. She was the State Regent for the DAR as well as being a registered nurse. She was an inspiration to other young women to join her profession. Kind and generous, yet she carried herself with elegance and propriety.

Aunt Betty married Uncle Harry who owned a jewelry store. My beautiful gold signet ring came from his store. Alas, one of my schoolmates stole it from me when I washed my hands. I've often wondered what girl wore an engraved "R" on her finger.

I rarely visited her house as a child except when my parents took me, but later was able to stay with her when I had a part-time job at the newspaper office in the summers. My bedroom was furnished with dark, elegant furniture. The bed was covered by a crisply pressed lace coverlet. The pillow covers had white designs made with French knots in a floral pattern. I remember the dark walnut mirror that hung on a stand with arms supporting it so it could swivel up and down.

My first impressions of her house as I entered her front door were of the stately staircase on the left leading to the second floor, its wood glowing with fresh polish. Her house number was 726, her car license was 726 and I think her phone number had 726 in it. The sitting room was filled with books; big books, small books, thick and thin books. I used to dream through her wealth of National Geographics while my parents talked of adult things. Some day when I grew up, I wanted to see those wonderful places. I was intrigued by her floor model Philco radio with lighted dial, housed in a polished walnut case. Sometimes she allowed me to play it.

In the dining room, a fine Chippendale table covered with a lace cloth was surrounded by matching chairs. There were neat piles of papers she was working on. She used to write devotions for Daily Blessing and did her research at that table.

I loved her kitchen—the old, off-white Philco refrigerator with the compressor on top that groaned when it started, her white table and chairs on top of a black and white ceramic square tiled floor. For breakfast, she would serve cold cereal and always pour milk or cream from a spotted cow pitcher. I inherited that pitcher. Although it has been broken and repaired several times, it is still has its charm. She had Toby mugs on her kitchen shelf. I used to think they were ugly but now realize they were very valuable.

When I returned to her house after work, we would walk through her sun porch and rose garden. Then she would always ask me if I'd like to go to The Dairy. Of course I would. The Dairy was about three blocks away across the railroad tracks. Aunt Betty would order a sandwich, and I would order a large chocolate malt. I have never found a better malted milk than The Dairy made.

When Aunt Betty died at ninety-seven, I was sad because there weren't many of her friends at her funeral. Then I realized that she had outlived them all. My life has been so much richer for having known my wonderful aunt who taught me honor, etiquette, history and how to relish the art of living.

COLLECTIONS

Mama had collections. I think it was hereditary. Her maiden aunties had collections, too. When we cleaned out Aunt Edna's attic, it took weeks to go through her collected magazines, articles and trinkets.

Mama collected old sheet music which she would vigorously play on the piano. She had a delightful collection of old valentines—the kind with red honeycomb folds inside. Some of them opened up into three dimension hearts, parasols, boats, or platforms for the valentine characters. She would let me look at them as she dug around in the old chest in the attic. That same chest held clothing made in the 1800's from ancient aunties on Papa's side. There were dark silk blouses, velvet vests, plaid taffeta skirts with cummerbunds and dresses with waists so tiny that they were not much larger than my biggest dolly.

The collection I liked the most was Mama's elephant collection. Whenever anyone traveled to a different state, they would bring her an elephant from that state. Her brother brought many from his travels around the Great Lakes and around the world. She had several from occupied Japan, real ivory ones from Africa that marched across a mahogany bridge, bronze, porcelain and wooden elephants. She had unusual, hard plastic balloon elephants with legs tied on with tiny strings. I believe she had at least one hundred-fifty elephants, some so tiny they could fit into a thimble and one large enough to hold two potted plants. Before Mama died, she said she wanted me to have her elephant collection. I treasured them and later added many more to their number.

THE TENT MEETING

"**O**uch, that hurt," I complained loudly as I scooted across the rough-hewn bench. I felt the splinter slice through my new nylons and into my thigh.

"Sh-h-h," Papa hissed at me and pointed to the speaker at the front." Eddie sat stiffly by my side.

I was sixteen and had never had a date. The girls in my class constantly talked about their dates, where they went and what they wore. One reason I had not dated was that no one except my cousin, Phil, had asked me to go out. The other reason was that my parents were afraid I'd go to some awful, wicked place on my date, like maybe a movie theater or a dance hall. I wasn't among the popular ones because I wasn't allowed to go anywhere exciting. I wasn't even allowed to go out to eat after a basketball game. I had to get the family car back home.

On day, after math class, Eddie asked me to go out with him. I had square-danced with him in the school gym over the noon hour. (I was forbidden to dance but who would tell?) He was from a strict Catholic family—a very nice guy, sort of shy and not bad looking. I had to ask my parents first. I wanted to make a new dress. I needed a new pair of high heels. I was so excited.

My Papa did not think I should be dating. Mama thought it would be a nice thing. Finally Papa said it would be all right, but that we had to go to a church meeting. My heart sank. Eddie, being Catholic, would not be allowed to go to our church.

Mama said, "But you could take him to the tent meeting."

"The tent meeting! What fun would that be!"

"Yes," said Papa, "I would allow you to go with him to the tent meeting."

I told Eddie the arrangement, and he agreed to take me. Brave soul that he was.

I found a pattern and made myself a new, quite fashionable two-piece dress, in a blue, green and purple flowered print. I talked Mama into getting me a new pair of shoes although I knew it cost her the milk money. A week was a long time to wait.

The great night of my date arrived. It was a hot August evening. I was allowed to ride with Eddie in his Chevy as we followed my parents. The meeting was held in a large tent supported by center poles, complete with sawdust floors and wooden benches. The music started with the pump organist playing a vigorous "There is Power in the Blood," and "Are You Washed in the Blood of the Lamb." I didn't dare to look at Eddie. But I could imagine just what he was thinking.

After a half hour of singing and sweating, the song leader gave up, and the evangelist started to preach. He was one of those hell-fire and brimstone preachers. As sweat dripped off his chin, he demanded "Hallelujah's" from the crowd. Waving his Bible in the air and striding from one side of the stage to the other, he pointed his finger at probable sinners.

The sermon droned on and on. Babies wiggled and cried. Little children ran in and out looking for the outhouse. Old men dozed—z-z-z-z-z. Perspiration ran down our faces and backs. Mosquitoes bit, and we slapped. Flies buzzed, and we swished. Poor Eddie, all he could do was wait for a way to escape.

Needless to say, he never asked me out again.

THE JOURNEY OF ANDREW MYERS

From the rugged slopes of Sweden
    Young Andrew Myers came,
The year eighteen and forty-three
    Eager to make his name.

He passed through Northern Ireland
    Caught up in national strife;
Met charming Marie Keller,
    Asked her to be his wife.

They married and hoped some day to raise
    Children that never came.
But when the potato famine hit,
    Ireland was not the same.

With his wife and their possessions
    They sailed for the New World,
Heard of a land of plenty with
    Freedom's promises unfurled.

His dear bride fell ill and worsened,
    "Lay me in free soil," she pled;
Young Andrew laid her down to rest,
    The New World her final bed.

Andrew continued on alone,
    His heart about to break;
He traveled inland heading west
    Found a riverboat to take.

Up the wide Ohio River
    Where Marietta lay,
He left the boat, hoisted his bag,
    Set off for a new day.

An Indian maid stood by the path,
    "I'll take your bags," said she,
Young Andrew fell for her soft brown eyes,
    "My woman you shall be!"

Her love produced four children fair
    Her praises they bestow,
On the mother of our lineage,
    But her name we do not know.

Rachel Kulp

Note: Andrew Myers was my great, great, great grandfather who married an unknown Indian maiden. Thus, I and my children have possible Indian blood in our veins.

MAMA'S HANDS

Mama's hands were helping hands, always doing good things for others. She worked hard on the farm for Papa and for us girls, so her hands were often rough and chapped. She cooked food for ailing neighbors and carried it to them with a word of encouragement. She never wore nail polish or had a manicure. Her wedding ring, a plain gold band worn very thin, was the only ring she ever wore. (After sixty years of marriage, it disappeared during her stay at the nursing home.) Those hands thinned carrots, weeded parsley, fed calves, changed diapers and rolled out the most delicious cookies and pies.

As years passed, I watched those wide, strong, capable hands slowly wrinkle and shrivel into small useless claws as rheumatoid arthritis consumed her body. She could no longer carry water to the cows, deliver food to the table or even feed herself. Others had to feed and dress her.

As the disease destroyed her body, her face became sweeter, and her spirit grew more beautiful. Instead of complaining, she pulled herself closer to her Savior and drew strength for each day from Him. Instead of being able to hold her children and grandchildren in those hands, she tightly held them in spirit and lifted them up to her Heavenly Father in daily prayer. Her hands were truly Blessed Hands.

LIKE MY MOM

My Mother was
A virtuous gal
Who loved her kids
And taught them well.

She cooked, she sewed
She fed the cows,
Hoed rows of corn
Stacked hay in mows

With face so soft
And voice so kind,
In each day's task
She honored God.

Though years have passed
And she is gone,
Wish I could say
"I love you, Mom."

By Rachel

THOSE FUNNY ROAD SIGNS

Advertising was very important even in the days before everyone had television. Enterprising companies devised many ways to promote their products to the public. Radio and newspapers carried the advertisements. Many times advertisers relied on jingles on the radio to sell their products. Contests were held to write the best jingle. That's how I won my first camera, a Brownie Hawkeye that I used for many years. Some of the more memorable jingles included:

> "Get Wildroot Hair Oil, Charley, (Hair tonic)
> It keeps your hair in trim.
> Get Wildroot Hair Oil, Charley,
> It's made with soothing Lan-o-lin."

Or

> "D-U-Z does everything" (Laundry powder)

Or

> "Bryll Crème (Hair groom)
> A little dab'll do ya.
> Bryll Crème
> You'll look so debonair."

All of these jingles were accompanied by a very catchy melody. The tunes were what sold the product. However, the most impressive advertisements were those funny road signs.

Our family would periodically drive to New Bavaria, Holgate or Ney to buy or sell grain. Those towns had elevators where grain was stored or ground. We would make a day of it. Mama would pack a simple picnic lunch that we would eat at some roadside park table. Sometimes we would take a jaunt to Bryan where some of Mama's relatives lived.

As we drove along, we would look for a series of red and white road signs on the right side of the road. There were always five signs in a row, placed about 100 feet apart. Each sign had one line of a four-line poem. The fifth sign always said "Burma Shave" in script. I remember some of those couplet poems that went like this:

"Don't kiss your girlfriend
At the gate,
Love may be blind
But the neighbors ain't.
Burma Shave.

Fuzzy Wuzzie was a bear
Fuzzy Wuzzie had no hair,
So Fuzzy Wuzzie
Wasn't (very) Fuzzy Wuzzie (Wuzzie).
Burma Shave

Within this vale
Of toil and sin,
Your head grows bald
But not your chin.
Burma Shave
Car in ditch,
Driver in tree,
Moon was full
And so was he.
Burma Shave

Around the curve,
Lickety Split.
Beautiful car
Wasn't it!
Burma Shave

Don't lose your head
To gain a minute
You need your head
Your brains are in it.
Burma Shave

Spring has sprung
The grass has riz
Over where last year's
Careless driver is.

(From The Verse By the Side of the Road by
Frank Rowsome, Jr.)

As fascinating as those signs were, they never convinced Papa to try the product. He was sold on lather and his old razor and strap.

BARN BUILDER

One of my favorite places on the farm was the barn. I loved the smell of it and the coziness of it even though it was very large inside. It smelled of fresh-mown hay, the feed mill, and the dusty beams. In the barn, kittens were born. They grew up and cleansed the building of mice. In the barn, six friendly cows chewed their cuds contentedly after they munched their daily ration of hay or grain in their stanchions waiting to be milked. Calves were born across from them in the birthing stalls and grew up to be our milkers or our table meat. As Mama and I milked the cows, barn swallows flew over our heads, tending their babies in their mud nest. Thirsty cats sat at a safe distance from the milking, waiting for us to flick a stream of milk in their direction. Pigeons cooed overhead from the center beams of the hay loft.

Papa designed the barn for our particular needs. Inside the door, on the right was the granary. Here, while Papa prepared for the next load, I would shovel off the wagon load of wheat or oats. There was space to store the wagon and our old '49 Ford sedan. The center section contained a large open space where we drove the hay wagon. Our barn was built sturdily with twelve-inch square beams supporting the center. The section for cows was on the left and led out to a fenced yard.

Until water lines were run to the barn, Mama would trudge daily from the pump to the barn, a full five-gallon bucket of water in each hand to water the cattle. It was back-breaking work. Before milking, we would clean the stalls, empty the manure and put in fresh bedding. I suppose the cows were grateful. At least they usually cooperated with Mama and me at milking time.

Papa was a barn builder. Only after I became an adult did I discover that he built many more barns than our own. In fact, he built the largest barn in Northwestern Ohio. That barn was pictured in Ohio's statewide bicentennial celebration in 2003.

In his later years, Papa had our barn painted. A painted barn was the sign of prosperity, and we certainly wanted to look prosperous, whether we were or not. Ohio barns were painted barn red with white trim. Papa ordered the job to be done. The painters charged him full price, and the barn looked fine as I drove into the yard. By this time, Papa was crippled and unable to inspect the job they had done.

I decided to have a look for myself. As I pushed the heavy sliding door open, I was astonished to see brilliant shafts of light pouring in. About one-half of the boards on the backside had fallen off. The painters didn't bother to replace them. They just painted the assorted boards that were still clinging to the beams, leaving great unboarded, unpainted gaps.

Papa's poor barn that looked so grand on the front side, on the back side looked like a lady in the wind whose full petticoat was showing to the world.

ENTERTAINMENT AND GADGETS

What did we do for entertainment in the early forties? When I was younger, I played with cut-out dolls. They came in books to cut out, dolls complete with many sets of clothing. We'd cut out the dolls and fasten their outfits on them with little tabs. Sometimes I'd swap outfits with my friends at school. I did a lot of imaginary stories with friends I made up because I didn't have any close neighbors.

There really wasn't a lot of time to play because, when I got older, I helped Papa a lot. When I had a chance, I read comic books over and over. We swapped those, too. My sister somehow had gotten the better collection. My favorites included: Flash Gordon, Archie (with Veronica and Betty), the Lone Ranger (I had lots of those), Gene Autry, and Roy Rogers. Of course there were lots of Walt Disney comics like Mickey and Minnie Mouse, Donald Duck and his nephews, Felix the Cat and other favorites.

Life would have been harder if we hadn't had gadgets. That's just what they were—helpful tools to get our work done:

The Potato Planter—We would cut potatoes in quarters so there was an eye in each piece. The potato planter was a three-foot wooden tube that had a metal door at the bottom. Papa would put a piece of potato into the tube, jam it into the ground with his foot, tilt it so the planter would open and drop the potato and then close itself. The potato was planted at just the right depth.

The Strainer—We got our soft water for washing from the rain barrel. The strainer was used to strain out the wigglers before we used the water.

The Apple Peeler and Cherry Pitter—Gadgets we used to get the fruit ready for Mama's delicious pies a whole lot quicker.

The Shoe Last—Papa would re-heel and re-sole our shoes so they would last and last.

The Electric Welder—Papa would repair most of our farm equipment himself. He said that the electric company was mad at him because the little meter dial on the welder went around so fast when he welded that they couldn't read it and charge him.

The Treadle Sewing Machine—Many happy hours were spent making my clothes, that is after I learned how to use it and not make holes in my finger.

Blue Jeans and Overalls—Only worn to slop the pigs and empty manure in the barn. Not to be seen on a female in mixed company and certainly not to wear to town.

The Apron—All mothers wore one. There were fancy ones when company came and simple bib styles for work at home. Most had pockets for handkies to wipe tears and noses.

The Flour Sifter—Used to make cakes and other baked goods more fluffy since self-rising flour wasn't invented yet. It folded out of our green kitchen cabinet and was attached to the bottom of the flour bin.

The Wash Tub—Not only was it used for the rinsing cycle of our wringer washer, but it also served as the Saturday night bathtub. We would put newspaper over all the windows. Mama would heat water on the cookstove and pour it into the tub. I always got the first use of the bath water. We used Fels Naptha soap on our bodies and hair and also on our clothes. No one had silky-smooth skin.

MORE ENTERTAINMENT

The Hoola Hoop—I never could master the silly things; they always ended up around my ankles.

The Early Radio—We'd gather in the evenings after work was done to listen to Papa's favorites like Walter Winchell, Amos and Andy, Radio Theater and the scary one—The Shadow Knows.

The Premiums—Stores and different products would give away little gifts tucked into their boxes or bags. Cracker Jack premiums were real games or statues. Duz included a piece of Depression glassware in every box. Other soaps included a piece of silver-plated silverware or a drinking glass. Cheerios packages held rings and baseball cards. Mama got her print of "The End of the Trail" as a Ten-Cent Store premium.

The Elvis Craze—My friends were crazy about Elvis and got tickets to see his movies. I was never allowed to go because Papa said the way he swiveled his hips was downright obscene. I could dream so I cut out the theater newspaper pictures from each of his movies and saved them in a scrapbook.

The Fifties Clothing—The Fifties had their own style of clothing. I had my own poodle-cloth wide circle skirt complete with black and white saddle shoes with pink soles. Saddles also came in brown and white. You were a nobody unless you had a pair of saddles.

The Black Seam—Our nylon stockings (worn with a garter belt) had a black seam down the back. It was a real challenge to keep those seams straight.

*   *   *

Mail and gasoline prices were low. Post cards cost 1 cent, letter stamps were 3 cents. Gas was a bargain at 33 cents a gallon. Even so, it was a struggle for poor farmers to fill their tanks.

LEFTOVERS

When Mama was in her kitchen, she cooked lots of food. She always planned for leftovers to eat for the next meal, and the next meal, and the next meal or until they were eaten. These are scraps and bits of leftovers to savor and enjoy.

*   *   *

Mama and Papa and I always went to church on Sundays. Even when we were sick or the cows got out, we eventually made it to church. We would often pick up someone who needed a ride. Often it was great Aunt Edna, or Auntie, as we knew her.

I remember one Sunday morning we picked her up in our 1937 Plymouth sedan and were exactly on time for church. We chatted as we rode along. Suddenly, Aunt Edna gave a loud gasp. "My teeth! My teeth!" she shouted. "I forgot my teeth!" We were late for church that day because we had to turn around and go back for her teeth.

*   *   *

Papa loved salt. I think part of the reason was that he worked in the fields and sweated a lot. When we sat at the table, Mama would place salt sellers beside each plate. A salt seller is a tiny glass bowl filled with large-grain salt. The ones she had were usually clear pressed glass for everyday and her pretty pressed green glass for Sundays. She would serve green onions, celery or carrots as greens. Papa would dunk each bite into his salt seller and relish the crunchy salt flavor.

*   *   *

I always felt lonely, especially since I was an only child for ten years. I needed a close friend. When I was almost ten, I finally understood what the preacher of our church was saying, that Jesus wanted me and loved me and was there to be my friend. I wanted Him too, and opened my heart and life to Him. Jesus has been my faithful friend, always by my side, ever since.

*   *   *

Mama would sometimes tell me things that happened in her childhood. Somewhere, back of Aunt Edna's house, was an abandoned railroad. The tracks were supposed to have led to Continental, Ohio. As kids, Mama and Uncle Paul used to walk those tracks, going as far as they could, but not so far that they couldn't get back in time for supper.

Mama was deathly allergic to anything fishy. Uncle Paul would go fishing in Powell's Creek and catch fish and crawdads. Then he would try to get Mama to hold his fish just so he could see her hands swell up. If someone fried fish in her presence, her throat would swell closed, and we would have to find a doctor quickly.

*   *   *

I liked most of our pet dogs, most of them except for the German Shepherd called Rex. My job was to feed him. I poured the feed into his bowl but didn't like where the bowl was sitting. I tried to move the bowl. Suddenly he was at my throat. I still have a scar where he went for my jugular. We never had another German Shepherd.

*   *   *

I liked my Uncle Harmon except when he liked to tease me. He knew I was afraid of snakes. This was probably because Mama was. She would not pet the dog if she knew the dog had just killed a snake. I always had to walk the cows down the lane to the woods for pasture. Uncle Harmon killed two blue racers and hung them in the tree along the lane, just over my head. He got a lot of pleasure watching me scream and run the cows under those trees to pasture.

*   *   *

When I was ten years old, Mama announced that I would be having a baby brother or sister. Of course Papa wanted a baby boy. I wanted a sister. Mama let me pat the baby in her tummy. It was a great adventure to help her care for my baby sister, after she was born. She was named after great Aunt Elizabeth and Mama's best friend. I didn't know what to do having a little person around. She followed me wherever I went. Sometimes it was a little annoying as I was used to being an only child. In later years I understood her better, and she and I became best friends.

*   *   *

Papa had a full array of outside equipment and tools inside. Outside, he had his prized Case tractor. He insisted that Case was the best kind. He had a three-bottom plow, disc, a harrow which the dog used to ride, corn planter, grain drill which doubled as a fertilizer spreader, manure spreader, old combine, hay mower and rake. Inside, he had a hand-turned corn sheller, a shoe tree or last that was used for repairing our shoes, and many hand tools. He hid his tools in a little bench which he sat on, beside the kitchen door. I will always remember his wide hands, his short, stubby fingers trying to repair a toy I had broken or a hole in Mama's enamelware. His solution for chipped enamelware pots was to insert a small screw topped by a nut into the hole and tighten. That explained the many scratches on Mama's stovetop. Papa was a very intelligent man and was able to repair most of our broken equipment.

*   *   *

My Mama was a teacher, at least for a little while. Whereas Papa only had an eighth grade education, Mama finished high school and took two years of college work. She wanted to get her degree so she could teach full-time but was not able because of farm duties. She loved to tutor and loved her students. She specialized in handicapped children. She had a little saying that I've always remembered when I was trying to achieve something:

> "Good, Better, Best.
> Never let it rest.
> Until your Good is better,
> And your Better best."

*   *   *

Mama loved green. Her home-made kitchen curtains were yellow and green. She was in a painting mood one day and painted the kitchen table, four chairs, Papa's kitchen bench, the tin cabinet for water glasses and the high chair (used by me and my sister) all milk-paint green with crème trim.

*   *   *

Outside the back door of the cement block house was a concrete step. Around the step were several bowls and jar lids. Mama would pour milk into the lids and bowls and break bread chunks into the milk. She would call "Kitty, kitty, kitty, kitty, here kitty, kitty." From their hiding places in the yard and barn, the cats would come. Calico cats, yellow cats, black and white cats. Her favorite was Winkie, the queen mother of cats. Winkie was a large calico. She had probably mothered close to one hundred kittens in her eight years of production. I remember having sixteen cats at one time around the back door. I would sit on that back step for hours enjoying the antics of her babies until I was given a job to do. Mama wrote many cat tales about the adventures of Winkie. The flies would also swarm around the cat pans. I didn't know about germs they brought so I just endured them.

*　　*　　*

Mama loved to play the piano. She also sang with a lovely alto voice. She was always disappointed that she was not a soprano because singing high notes was supposed to be more honorable. We sang hymns together after supper dishes were washed. Because she was the official pianist for Highland Grange, Mama wanted me to learn piano so she paid for lessons out of her grocery money. I was the only piano student among the thirty accordion students my teacher had. This teacher was selected to teach me because she charged less than other teachers.

Mama was thrilled when I was asked to sing my first solo in church. I was in the eighth grade. She somehow got a new outfit for me including a light green sheer dress with white flocking, new shoes and my first pair of nylons. I remember trying not to be frightened at the congregation as I sang. So, I pretended they were all cabbage heads.

*　　*　　*

Papa's talent was playing the violin. Actually, he played it as a fiddle and had a small repertoire including "Old Black Joe," "Oh Susannah," and other Negro spirituals. I think he purchased his violin in the 1920's when he had money from working on the construction crew. He was quite proud that he could play although he hardly ever practiced. When company came, he would put resin on the bow, tune it and play with a cute, proud, little twisted grin on his face.

I did enjoy hearing the dramatic recitations he gave in the Negro dialect. There were some very funny stories in his drama book. I didn't mind hearing them over and over. Sometimes a Sunday School class or the Grange would ask him to perform as part of their programs.

*　　*　　*

There were little joys in daily living. Little things like squirting the cats with milk as I milked the cows. Or, watching the barn swallows dart back and forth, catching mosquitoes to feed their babies in the nest overhead.

On the Fourth of July, I always asked Papa if we could go and see fireworks. He usually said he had grain to harvest or some other project to do that would take him well into the night. I remember one time when he said no after my pleading. I just had to have some Fourth of July "noise". I took a big long stick and went to the steel corncrib. I pounded so long and loud that I'm surprised the neighbors didn't call the sheriff. At least we had noise.

*   *   *

I wanted to help with the family food supplies. I figured that if I had a good bow and arrows, I could probably shoot rabbits and maybe a deer or two. Finally, Papa took me to the woods where we selected a straight hickory branch about five and one-half feet long. Papa said he would make a bow for me after the wood had seasoned. Each year I would ask him if it was seasoned enough. He would say it wasn't. It must have needed a lot of seasoning because after twenty years, that piece of wood was still there.

*   *   *

When I was in grade school, I wanted to play baseball with the big kids. Since I was an only child for so long, I wanted to fit in with a group so I went to their games. I decided I would help the catcher retrieve the ball during batting practice before a game. The catcher missed the first ball. I bent over to pick up the ball. The pitcher immediately threw again. "Bonk!" the ball struck me on the very top of my head and bounced to the ground with a dull thud. I probably acted very strange for a while, at least until the lump went down.

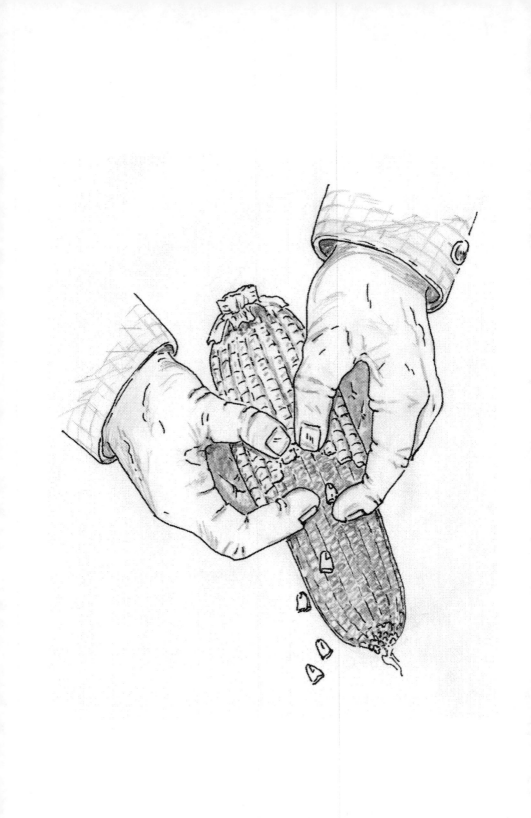

CONCLUSION—
THE CORNSHELLER

Years have passed and the new house is now an old house. Mama has passed on and Papa lived to over one-hundred and one. I remember a scene from days when Papa had to live alone in that big house and forage for himself:

I saw him as I peered into the kitchen. There he sat, hunched over in his chair, concentrating on what he was doing. His bald head was wrinkled with sparse gray, once red, hairs straggling above his ears and longer around the back. He seemed so old, almost eternal. Papa had aged considerably since I last saw him. His tall, sturdy frame had shrunk to less than five feet and many lines caressed his face.

I looked at his hands, wide hands. They were gnarly with ancient freckles dotted across them. His stubby fingers moved unceasingly across the dried corn, freeing the kernels, leaving neat cob rows. The pile of yellow kernels grew higher. He did not hear me or see me. His eyesight was fading and his hearing had nearly diminished. I watched until the golden bowl was full.

With a groan, he raised himself off the chair and, using his crutches for support, hobbled across to the sink, carrying the bowl. I knew he would grind the corn and make himself cornmeal for several breakfasts.

He was all alone, lonely for his wife who had long ago passed on to brighter days, surrounded by things familiar to him—his farm, his books, his habits. He had no one to wash for him, no one to cook for him. I knew it sometimes took several hours just to make just one meal. Somehow he would keep on going, one endless day at a time, one slow step at a time until the end. He had courage. He had spunk.

His kitchen was dingy and poorly lit, with cupboards cluttered by cracked cups and worn silverware. The once yellow and green-flowered wallpaper Mama had loved above the blackened cook stove was grungy brown from decades of grease spatters. The battered wood cabinets piled high to the ceiling had not seen a scrub rag since Mama died.

I wished I could bring back yesterday with its youth and vitality for him. Yet, as I watched the pile of yellow corn kernels grow, I knew there was always hope for tomorrow.

The era of pre-electricity is gone. We could not live well now without our electric lights and appliances, computers, and the advances in electronics and medicine. Yet the morals and character built into the lives of folks who learned "to do without" are to be envied. Stability, kindness, honesty, and bonds between neighbors were assumed back in that era. How we lived and survived in that pre-modern time still amazes me. We dare never forget the joys and sorrows we shared then. We were Living on the Edge of an Era.